Oxford *Smart*

QUEST 1
ENGLISH LANGUAGE AND LITERATURE

Helen Backhouse
Jane Branson
Sarah Eggleton

OXFORD
UNIVERSITY PRESS

Contents

Welcome to Quest!		4
Using the Quest Student Book		5
Plan, Monitor, Evaluate		6

Chapter 1: Texts all around us — 8

Learning overview — 10

Unit	Source text	Skill	Page
1.1 When is a text a text?	• Captain Scott letter • 'How not to care what other people think of you' blog by Tavi Gevinson	Reading	12
1.2 What is a poem?	• 'I Want a Poem' by Shukria Rezaei • 'The Factory' by Letitia Elizabeth Landon	Writing	18
1.3 What's the story?	• Two boys lost in the Amazon article • *Pigeon English* by Stephen Kelman	Reading	24
1.4 Why all the drama?	• *Romeo and Juliet* by William Shakespeare • *Here Be Dragons* by Jordan Cobb	Writing	30
1.5 What is a classic text?	• *The Lion, the Witch and the Wardrobe* by C.S. Lewis	Reading	36
1.6 How is your voice heard?	• 'The Danger of a Single Story' by Chimamanda Ngozi Adichie	Speaking	42
1.7 Which English do you speak?	• 'Running' by Benjamin Zephaniah • Article by Benjamin Zephaniah	Writing	48
1.8 What's the right tone?	• Speech to the UN by Malala Yousafzai • Air Ambulance charity website	Reading	54

Contents

Chapter 2: Crime and consequences — 60

Learning overview — 62

Unit		Source text	Skill	Page
2.1	Why do we love crime fiction?	• 'Four Reasons We Love Binging Crime Shows' • Crime fiction blurbs	Writing	64
2.2	What makes a character?	• 'The Murders in the Rue Morgue' by Edgar Allan Poe	Reading	70
2.3	Who's telling the story?	• *Smart* by Kim Slater	Writing	76
2.4	Why all the tension?	• *Murder in Midwinter* by Fleur Hitchcock	Reading	82
2.5	What's the news?	• Model railway destroyed article	Writing	88
2.6	What is figurative language?	• 'Stealing' by Carol Ann Duffy • 'Guilty Conscience' by Sagar Garg	Reading	94
2.7	What's the difference?	• *A Day in the Life of a Prisoner* by Michael Romero • *My Fifteen Lost Years* by Florence Maybrick	Reading	100
2.8	Can a text change your mind?	• 'Who should get credit for declining youth crime?' by Ally Fog	Speaking	106

Chapter 3: Journeys and discoveries — 112

Learning overview — 114

Unit		Source text	Skill	Page
3.1	How do journeys create jeopardy?	• *The Body* by Stephen King	Reading	116
3.2	What is a quest?	• *Medusa* by Jessie Burton	Writing	122
3.3	Why start with a journey?	• *Jamaica Inn* by Daphne du Maurier	Reading	128
3.4	How can poetry explore journeys?	• 'Things We Carry on the Sea' by Wang Ping	Reading	134
3.5	What is travel writing?	• Blog post by Alastair Humphreys	Writing	140
3.6	Why travel sustainably?	• Sustainable holidays article	Speaking	146
3.7	Why take a risk?	• 'Bungee at Victoria Falls: The Day the Void Came for Me' by Deborah O'Donoghue	Writing	152
3.8	Can journeys tell stories?	• *Brown Girl Dreaming* by Jacqueline Woodson	Reading	158

Key terms glossary	**164**
Boosting your vocabulary glossary	**166**

3

Welcome to Quest!

Quest delivers the 11–14 segment of the Oxford Smart Curriculum Service for English and has been written to:

- build on the variety of learner experiences at KS2 and explore English as a unique discipline, empowering, engaging and motivating both learners and teachers
- support teachers in delivering a diverse, relevant and challenging curriculum
- look back across the rich literary heritage of English Literature but also forwards to a future dominated by the digital world
- allow teachers to identify and address misconceptions and misunderstandings
- provide access to high-quality texts from a wide range of writers, both classic and contemporary, and from a range of backgrounds, cultures and experiences
- offer flexibility and choice while still delivering the core skills and knowledge so that teachers can customise their route through the resources
- enable efficient and effective progress tracking, giving teachers the confidence that students will be ready to embark on their GCSE studies by the end of Year 9.

Course overview

Student Books

Quest includes digital and printed Student Books for each year of KS3. Book 1 builds on the knowledge students have from KS2 and introduces them to a wide variety of texts and themes, while laying the foundation for future English study. Books 2 and 3 develop students' knowledge and skills further and prepare them for English at KS4.

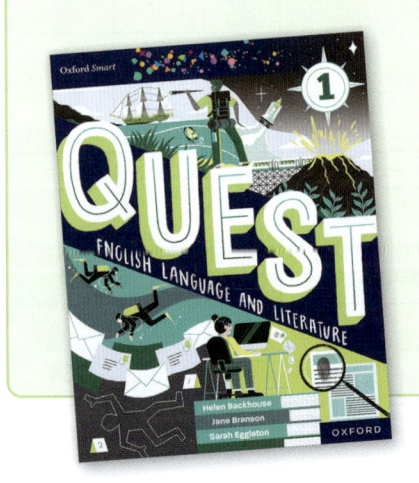

Teacher Books

Digital and printed Teacher Books help support the planning and implementation of Quest. Each of the three Teacher Books contains introductions to the Student Book topics, flexible lesson plans with unit-by-unit guidance, additional activity ideas, assessment support, further reading suggestions, plus tips on how to integrate the Kerboodle resources into your lessons.

Kerboodle

Oxford Smart Quest Kerboodle provides access to digital versions of the Student Books and Teacher Books, additional teaching and learning resources, as well as a comprehensive assessment package. Resources include worksheets with alternative texts, audio recordings of source texts, answers to Student Book activities, automatically marked assessments, as well as a CPD and Research Hub that includes a wealth of resources to support your professional development.

Using the Quest Student Book

In each chapter

Chapter opener: Each chapter in the Student Book starts with a chapter opener that activates prior knowledge and informs students about what they will be learning.

Learning overview: The learning overview supports metacognition by preparing students for what they will be learning and will help them to monitor what they have learned. It also shows a coherent learning pathway through the Student Book.

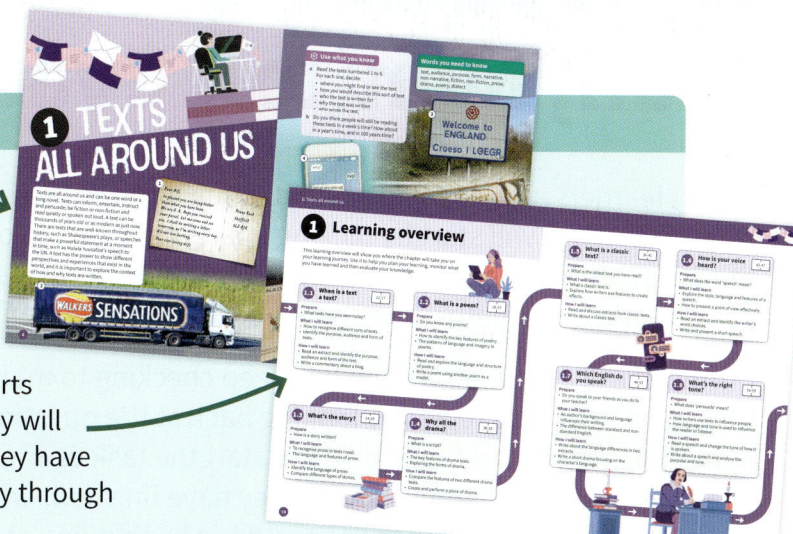

In each unit

Learning objectives focus on what students will be learning and how they will demonstrate their understanding. The first objective is about what the student will learn, the second is about what they are exploring, investigating or considering further and the third objective is to write, analyse or present what they have learned.

What's the big idea? gives an overview of what the unit is about and why it is important. It can also include links to previous units as a reminder of what students already know.

⭐ Boosting your vocabulary

Boosting your vocabulary sections provide activities and strategies to help students work out unfamiliar Tier 2 words from the source texts, along with opportunities for them to practise using the words in their own writing.

💡 Building your knowledge

Building your knowledge sections introduce the knowledge focus of each unit in the context of the source text. Students are encouraged to think about what they already know and understand about the focus of the unit, drawing on their own experiences.

🧩 Putting it all together

Putting it all together sections conclude each unit. The tasks in the unit build towards students completing a final activity that will allow them to demonstrate that they can apply the skills and knowledge covered.

Features

✅ **Tips** remind students of a connection to another key piece of knowledge or key skill and give prompts.

❓ **Did you know?** offers short and snappy facts to aid or add to students' comprehension of a text.

🔑 **Key terms** are flagged the first time they appear in a chapter and include technical or literary terms. A complete glossary of key terms is included at the end of each Student Book.

⬆ **Stretch yourself** activities encourage students to think in more depth or to take their learning further in order to expand their knowledge and develop their skills.

✏ **Writing icons** indicate when students are expected to write their answer or response to the activity.

5

Welcome to Quest!

Plan, Monitor, Evaluate

Expert learners approach new and unfamiliar tasks in a structured way. Often, they will start by picking apart the question or task, thinking carefully about what subject knowledge or skill they are going to need or whether they have seen something similar before.

During a task an expert learner will keep checking to make sure they are on track by regularly looking back at the question. Sometimes they may even decide to start the task again and choose a different approach. After they have finished, an expert learner will reflect on how they have done by thinking about any areas of improvement and putting a plan together for what they would do differently next time.

The Plan, Monitor, Evaluate cycle is a structure you can follow to help you approach a new task like an expert learner. This cycle should be used every time you complete a task.

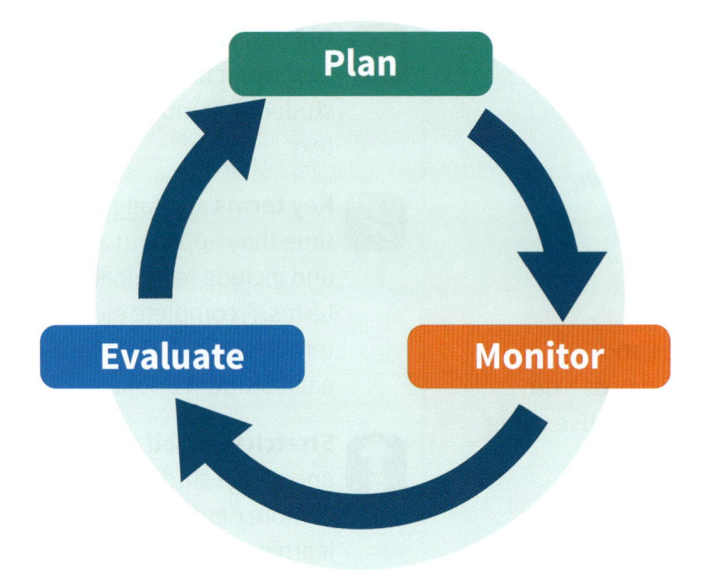

Activity

Discuss your answers to these questions:

a   When does the planning phase take place?

b   How can you monitor your progress during the monitoring phase?

c   Why is the evaluation phase important?

Plan, Monitor, Evaluate

Plan

The planning phase takes place **before** you start the task. This is where you plan your approach to the task by thinking about what you already know and what pieces of information relate to the task.

Here some examples of the types of questions you could be asking yourself before you start a new task.

- How many marks does this question have?
- What knowledge or skill do I need to recall to answer the question?
- Have I answered a similar question before? What did success look like then?
- What have I learnt from the examples my teacher has shown me?

Evaluate

When you have completed a task, it is important to reflect on how you have done. An expert learner learns from their mistakes and uses teacher feedback to move their own learning forward.

Here are some examples of the types of questions you should be asking yourself after a task.

- What went well?
- Did I miss any marks? If so, for what?
- Is there any other strategy that I could have used to complete this task?
- What areas do I need to improve upon for next time?

Monitor

Once you have started the task it is important to monitor your own progress. Sometimes by pausing and reviewing the task you may choose to change your approach. You may even decide that you need to go back and re-read some content to help you complete the task.

Here are some examples of the types of questions you should be asking yourself during a task.

- How do I feel now that I am answering the question? Confident or unsure?
- Am I meeting the requirements of the task or question?
- Do I need to stop and change anything I have done?
- Have I followed the examples that my teacher has shown me?

1 TEXTS ALL AROUND US

Texts are all around us and can be one word or a long novel. Texts can inform, entertain, instruct and persuade; be fiction or non-fiction and be read quietly or spoken out loud. A text can be thousands of years old or as modern as just now. There are texts that are well-known throughout history, such as Shakespeare's plays, or speeches that make a powerful statement at a moment in time, such as Malala Yousafzai's speech to the UN. A text has the power to show different perspectives and experiences that exist in the world, and it is important to explore the context of how and why texts are written.

1

Dear Alf,

So pleased you are doing better than you have been.
We are O.K. Hope you received your parcel. Let me come and see you. I shall be writing a letter tomorrow, as I'm writing every day.
All our love darling,
Your ever-loving wife

Penny Road
Sheffield
SL2 8JK

2

WALKERS SENSATIONS

Use what you know

a Read the texts numbered 1 to 6. For each one, decide:
- where you might find or see the text
- how you would describe this sort of text
- who the text is written for
- why the text was written
- who wrote the text.

b Do you think people will still be reading these texts in a week's time? How about in a year's time, and in 100 years' time?

Words you need to know

text, audience, purpose, form, narrative, non-narrative, fiction, non-fiction, prose, drama, poetry, dialect

3 Welcome to ENGLAND / Croeso i LOEGR

4 Text message conversation:
- Hey!
- Hey!
- What are you up to tomorrow?
- Nothing. Shall we go to the cinema? 😊
- Yes, I'm free after 2 o'clock
- Great!

5 The Tyger

Tyger Tyger, burning bright,
In the Forests of the night;
What immortal hand or eye,
Could frame thy fearful symmetry?

In what distant deeps or skies.
Burnt the fire of thine eyes?
On what wings dare he aspire?
What the hand, dare seize the fire?

And what shoulder, & what art,
Could twist the sinews of thy heart?
And when thy heart began to beat.
What dread hand? & what dread feet?

What the hammer? what the chain,
In what furnace was thy brain?
What the anvil? What dread grasp.
Dare its deadly terrors clasp?

When the stars threw down their spears
And water'd heaven with their tears:
Did he smile his work to see?
Did he who made the Lamb make thee?

Tyger Tyger burning bright,
In the Forests of the night:
What immortal hand or eye,
Dare frame thy fearful symmetry?

6 NADIYA BAKES — Over 100 must-try recipes for breads, cakes, biscuits, pies, and more — NADIYA HUSSAIN, The Great British Baking Show

FOOD × FIRE — GRILLING AND BBQ WITH DEREK WOLF, OVER THE FIRE COOKING

1: Texts all around us

1 Learning overview

This learning overview will show you where the chapter will take you on your learning journey. Use it to help you plan your learning, monitor what you have learned and then evaluate your knowledge.

1.1 When is a text a text? | 12–17

Prepare
- What texts have you seen today?

What I will learn
- How to recognise different sorts of texts.
- Identify the purpose, audience and form of texts.

How I will learn
- Read an extract and identify the purpose, audience and form of the text.
- Write a commentary about a blog.

1.2 What is a poem? | 18–23

Prepare
- Do you know any poems?

What I will learn
- How to identify the key features of poetry.
- The patterns of language and imagery in poems.

How I will learn
- Read and explore the language and structure of poetry.
- Write a poem using another poem as a model.

1.3 What's the story? | 24–29

Prepare
- How is a story written?

What I will learn
- To recognise prose in texts I read.
- The language and features of prose.

How I will learn
- Identify the language of prose.
- Compare different types of stories.

1.4 Why all the drama? | 30–35

Prepare
- What is a script?

What I will learn
- The key features of drama texts.
- Different forms of drama.

How I will learn
- Compare the features of two different drama texts.
- Create and perform a piece of drama.

1.5 What is a classic text? 36–41

Prepare
- What is the oldest text you have read?

What I will learn
- What a classic text is.
- How writers create character.

How I will learn
- Read and discuss an extract from a classic text.
- Write about a classic text.

1.6 How is your voice heard? 42–47

Prepare
- What does the word 'speech' mean?

What I will learn
- The style, language and features of a speech.
- How to present a point of view effectively.

How I will learn
- Read an extract and identify the writer's word choices.
- Write and present a short speech.

1.7 Which English do you speak? 48–53

Prepare
- Do you speak to your friends as you do to your teacher?

What I will learn
- An author's background and language influences their writing.
- The difference between Standard and non-standard English.

How I will learn
- Write about the language differences in two extracts.
- Write a short drama focusing on the characters' language.

1.8 What's the right tone? 54–59

Prepare
- What does 'persuade' mean?

What I will learn
- How writers craft texts to influence people.
- How language and tone is used to influence the reader or listener.

How I will learn
- Read a speech and change the tone of how it is spoken.
- Write about a speech and analyse the purpose and tone.

11

1: Texts all around us

1.1 When is a text a text?

In this unit, you will:
- learn to recognise different sorts of text
- understand how to identify the purpose, audience and form of a text
- write about a text, commenting on its key features.

What's the big idea?

There are texts everywhere: in books and magazines; on posters and adverts; in letters and diaries; in messages on smartphones and online on websites; in recipes and instruction sheets; even on road signs and on the backs of buses. People can see different types of texts everywhere they go.

What do all these texts have in common, and what are the differences between them?

Activity 1

a   List all the **texts** you have come across so far today.

b   How many other types of text can you think of?

c   What are the shortest and the longest texts you can think of?

Building your knowledge

There are three important features that you should focus on for all texts: **form**, **audience** and **purpose**.

Sometimes, when reading a text, these features are not obvious, and you have to act like a detective to work out what sort of text it is, who the audience is and the reason it was written. There are clues in every text if you know where to look.

Key terms

audience the people or person for whom a text is written or performed

form the organisation of writing in a particular way, e.g. a letter or a poem

purpose the reason that a text is written

text any form of written material

Tip

Remember that some texts have an audience of thousands or even millions; others have an audience of just one or two people.

1.1: When is a text a text?

Purpose and form

There are many different purposes (reasons) that a writer might have to create a text.

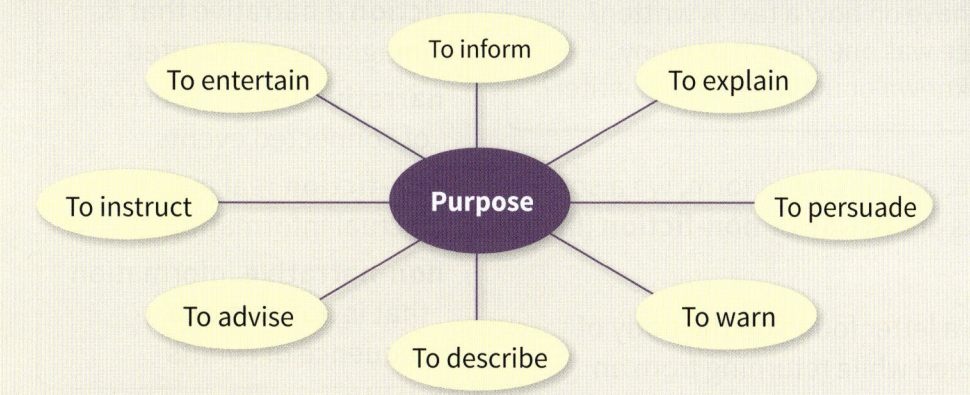

Purpose:
- To inform
- To entertain
- To explain
- To instruct
- To persuade
- To advise
- To warn
- To describe

> **Tip**
>
> Remember that some texts can have more than one purpose. For example, they could advise and instruct, or persuade and argue.

Activity 2

Think of an example of a text type (form) to match each of the purposes above. Explain each choice. An example has been completed below.

> To advise – a recipe guide to balanced eating. This gives the reader advice about how a range of different foods benefit you.

Audience

Think about the audience for a text. Texts can be sent as letters in the post, via instant messaging on a smartphone to a single person, or posted online for millions to read. Texts can be published in books and magazines, bought from shops or online, borrowed from the library, or they can be written on street signs, in adverts or in shop windows for people to read.

Activity 3

With a partner, discuss some of the different places you might come across a text, what type of texts they might be and who the texts might be written for. Some ideas have been included below.

Where (location)	What (text type)	Who (audience)	Why (purpose)
bus shelter	advert	people who live nearby	to persuade
library	picture books	children	to entertain

13

1: Texts all around us

> ## ⬆ Stretch yourself
> What impact does the audience have on how a text is written? How would it differ if the audience was one person or many people? Or if the audience were known or unknown to the writer?

🔑 Key terms

fiction a narrative that is imaginary or invented

narrative a story or account of connected events

non-fiction real events or factual information

non-narrative information that is not part of a sequence of events

As well as thinking about purpose, audience and form, we also need to think about whether texts are **fiction** or **non-fiction** (fact), **narrative** or **non-narrative**.

Read the extract below. It is from a letter found on the body of the explorer Captain Scott, who died while returning from an expedition to reach the South Pole in 1912.

Form — This text is in the form of a letter.

Audience — The letter was written to Scott's wife, although many others have read it since.

Narrative — The letter tells the story of the sad progress of the expedition.

Purpose — The purpose was to explain why he was unlikely to return, and to reassure her that his death would be 'painless'.

Extract from Captain Scott's last letter to his wife

To: My widow

Dearest darling — we are in a very **tight corner** and I have doubts of pulling through [...] We have **gone downhill** a good deal since I wrote the above. Poor Titus Oates has gone — he was in a bad state — the rest of us keep going and imagine we have a chance to get through but the cold weather doesn't let up at all [...]

Since writing the above we have got to within 11 miles of our **depot** with one hot meal and two days cold food and we should have got through but have been held for four days by a frightful storm — I think the best chance has gone we have decided to fight it to the last for that depot but in the fighting there is a painless end so don't worry.

tight corner – difficult situation
gone downhill – things have got worse
depot – a place which holds supplies

Non-fiction — The details in the letter and evidence of the expedition suggest the events were true.

14

1.1: When is a text a text?

Activity 4

a How do you think Captain Scott might have felt writing this letter?

b How do you think his wife Kathleen might have felt receiving the letter?

c Write a short paragraph to explain what you understand about their thoughts and feelings. You could use these sentence starters:

> I think Captain Scott must have felt desperately lonely because he knew that...

> I imagine that when Kathleen read her husband's letter, she felt...

Activity 5

Write your own short letter to describe a dramatic event. It could be fiction or non-fiction. Think about your audience and your purpose, and what you will or won't include.

Make sure your letter includes:

- a date
- a greeting
- an account of what happened
- an explanation of how you felt
- an ending with good wishes
- a signature.

You could start by writing:

> 27th April 1973
>
> Dear Charlie,
> You will never guess what has happened today! I still cannot believe it. Only you will understand how terrified I was.
> I was just walking along the street, on my way to the shops, when suddenly...

1: Texts all around us

Read the text below. It is a text written by Tavi Gevinson, who started blogging about fashion at 11 years old. At 14, she started her own online magazine for teenagers.

> **Extract from 'How not to care what other people think of you' by Tavi Gevinson**
>
> Some people think that once you start dressing 'weirdly', you have to keep it up. My middle school reputation was based on wearing really crazy stuff, and whenever I went to school in PJs, some people thought I'd given in to the **naysayers**. If anyone said anything, I just had to shrug and be like, **naw** man, I'm tired today. Again, it's about the whole people-deciding-your-image-for-you thing. Don't let them. Make them feel stupid for trying. This might feel cruel at first, but have no shame or guilt. You have every right to wear whatever you want, and if someone is so narrow-minded that they need to get on you about it so that the world is easier for them to understand, they might need a reminder that it doesn't work that way.
>
> ---
>
> **naysayers** – people who are negative. Literally it means 'no sayers'; people who say no
> **naw** – American slang for 'no'

⭐ Boosting your vocabulary

Writers choose their words carefully. The activity below focuses on some key vocabulary in the source text, which has been highlighted above.

Activity 6

a Having a reputation means a number of people have opinions about you. Using the word 'reputation', write a sentence to explain Tavi's reputation with the students at her school.

b 'Shame' and 'guilt' are **abstract nouns**. They are both emotions. Write a list of as many abstract nouns as you can think of. Think about other emotions to get you started.

c The **compound word** 'narrow-minded' means that someone is not prepared to listen to or consider other people's opinions or viewpoints. Below are some more compound words that can be used to describe other parts of the body.

   flat-footed   soft-hearted   wide-eyed

Create three hyphenated compound words of your own and write a sentence for each to show your understanding.

> 🔑 **Key terms**
>
> **abstract noun** a noun that refers to an idea, quality or emotion, rather than a solid object, e.g. *happiness, truth, freedom*
>
> **compound word** a word that is made up of two or more other words. Some compound words have hyphens, but not all, e.g. *ear-splitting, suitcase, hedgehog*

1.1: When is a text a text?

Putting it all together

Activity 7

Answer the following questions and try to find evidence from the text to support your point of view. The first question about the audience has been done for you.

a Who is the audience for the text?

> I think the audience is young people because the writer uses informal language and slang which teenagers would use like 'naw man'. I think the audience could be general because it is posted online where everyone can see it. I also think it is for teenagers of any gender because it doesn't say one or the other.

✓ Tip

See how the example answer uses 'because' to explain the point of view. In your own answers, try using 'because' or similar words or phrases.

b What is the writer's purpose in the text?

c Is the text narrative or non-narrative?

d Do you think the text is fiction or non-fiction?

e The writer chose to write this text as a blog. Why do you think blogs are a popular form of text that many writers and readers engage with?

Activity 8

How would you explain Tavi's point of view in her blog? How does she feel about the clothes she wears and the impact they have on other people?

Comment on how she appeals to her young audience (including her choice of form), and how successful she is in achieving her purpose.

17

1: Texts all around us

1.2 What is a poem?

In this unit, you will:
- learn about some of the key features of poetry
- discover patterns of language and imagery in poems
- write a poem, building on a modelled structure.

What's the big idea?

In the first unit, you learned that texts have an audience and a purpose, and are written in different forms. You also learned that texts can be fiction or non-fiction and they can be narrative or non-narrative. In English lessons, you explore a wide range of different texts, but they are mostly in the form of poetry, prose or drama.

In this unit, we will look at **poetry**.

People have been creating poems for thousands of years to express feelings in a creative way and to share a response to events happening around them. Why are people still inspired to share poems today? What exactly makes poems different from **prose** and **drama**?

Activity 1

Some people believe that poetry and songs are very similar forms. Think about some songs and poems that you know.

a How are they the same?

b How are they different?

c Do you think poems and songs are fiction or non-fiction? Explain your answer and give some examples.

Key terms

drama a play written for performance on stage or to be listened to

poetry a piece of writing often arranged in short lines and stanzas, following a pattern of sounds, and expressing feelings and ideas with great imagination

prose written language in its ordinary form, rather than poetry or drama

repetition using the same word or phrase more than once

stanza a group of lines in a poem with a line space before and after it

In this unit, you will explore two poems. You will learn about some of the key features of poetry and how these create a powerful effect for the reader.

1.2: What is a poem?

The poem below was written by a 15-year-old student, Shukria Rezaei. She was born in Afghanistan but came to England as a refugee when she was 14. Her poem describes how she feels about poetry.

> **Tip**
>
> Read the poem aloud and think about how the words *sound* as you say them.

'I Want a Poem' by Shukria Rezaei

I want a poem
with the texture of a **colander**
on the pastry.

A verse
5   of pastry so rich
it leaves gleam on your fingertips.

A poem
that stings like the splash of boiling oil
as you drop the pastry in.

10 A poem
that sits on a silver plate with
nuts and chocolates, served up to guests who
sit cross legged on the **thoshak**.

A poem
15 as vibrant as our **saffron** tea
served up at Eid.

Let your poetry
texture the blank paper
like a prism splitting light.

20 Don't leave without seeing all the colours.

---

colander – a bowl with holes in it for washing or draining food
thoshak – a floor cushion or narrow mattress that is commonly used in Afghanistan as a sofa to sit and eat on
saffron – a spice used in cooking or for health benefits

Activity 2

a   What patterns can you see in the way the poem is laid out? Think about the splitting into **stanzas**, the **repetition**, where the pattern changes slightly towards the end of the poem.

b   In each stanza, the poet creates a different image in your mind. Describe these images.

c   Which senses do you think the poet is trying to appeal to? Think about sight, sound, touch, taste and smell.

d   What mood does the poem create? You could use some of the words below in your answer.

fearful   excited   proud   calm   yearning

violent   intense   contented

1: Texts all around us

⭐ Boosting your vocabulary

Writers choose their words carefully. The activity below focuses on some key vocabulary in the source text, which has been highlighted on page 19.

Activity 3

a   The word 'gleam' means a soft light, as if polished. Choose words from the coloured boxes below to write a sentence describing how each of these things might shine:
   i   the moon
   ii a star
   iii a match
   iv a car headlight in the rain.

   flashed   beamed   glittered   glinted   gleamed

   shimmered   glowed   twinkled   flared

   The first one has been done for you.

   The moon gleamed in the inky black sky.

b   The words 'rich' and 'gleam' create a feeling of luxury, comfort and beauty. What effect does the word 'stings' have, in contrast?

c   Describe what a prism does to light. Look at the picture to help you.

d   Find the word 'prism' in the poem. How does your description help you to understand what the writer is saying about poetry?

e   The word 'vibrant' can mean bold and strong. Think of two words which mean the opposite of vibrant. Write a sentence using 'vibrant' and one of your chosen words.

1.2: What is a poem?

Building your knowledge

A good poem makes an impact on the reader. It conveys an idea in an interesting way, playing with word patterns, sounds and ideas.

When exploring poetry, think about how the poet has crafted their poem. As we explored in 'I Want a Poem', think about:
- the layout of the poem; how the poet has divided up their ideas
- how the poet has introduced patterns of sound and repetition
- what pictures have been created in our mind
- how words and images appeal to different senses
- what the overall mood of the poem is
- what the main message of the poem is.

Imagery and comparisons

Many poets use striking imagery to entertain their readers and to encourage them to think of things in a different way. Shukria Rezaei creates images by using comparisons to describe a perfect poem. She uses the theme of creating a feast for guests and creates **similes** and **metaphors** to draw comparisons.

Look at how the poet uses a metaphor in the stanza below.

> A verse
> of pastry so rich
> it leaves gleam on your fingertips.

— She compares a verse of poetry to pastry.

— Poetry and pastry are described as 'rich' — full, tasty, sweet and plentiful.

— She compares the gleaming oil from the pastry which is left on her fingers to the lasting effect of a poem which is left on the reader.

Did you know?

The ancient Greek poet Plutarch agreed that poems are all about pictures in your head. Two thousand years ago he said, "Painting is silent poetry, and poetry is painting that speaks."

Key terms

metaphor a comparison that says one thing *is* something else, e.g. *Amy was a rock*

simile a comparison of one thing to another, using *as* or *like*, e.g. *He swam like a fish*

Activity 4

a Look at the fourth stanza. How does the poet suggest that a poem is valuable, and to be shared and enjoyed with friends?

b Look at how the poet uses a simile in the fifth stanza by comparing a poem to something as colourful and spicy as saffron tea. Find another stanza in the poem that uses a simile, and explain what it suggests.

c Write your own stanza for this poem with your own simile. Follow the same structure as the stanzas mentioned above.

1: Texts all around us

Some poems are personal, like Shukria Rezaei's poem which is about her feelings and her identity. Other poems are about bigger, public issues such as politics or historical events.

Two hundred years ago, the poem below was written about the terrible lives of children working in factories in Britain. Although the subject is very different from the first poem, this poem can still be explored in a similar way.

'The Factory' by Letitia Elizabeth Landon

There rests a shade above **yon** town,
A dark **funereal shroud**:
'Tis not the tempest hurrying down,
'Tis not a summer cloud.
5 The smoke that rises on the air
Is as a type and sign;
A shadow flung by the despair
Within those streets of thine.

That smoke shuts out the cheerful day,
10 The sunset's purple **hues**,
The moonlight's pure and tranquil ray
The morning's pearly dews.

There rises on the morning wind
A low appalling cry,
15 A thousand children are **resigned**
To sicken and to die!

yon – (yonder) that … over there
funereal shroud – a cloth used to wrap a dead body
hues – colours
resigned – accepting that something bad will happen

Activity 5

a Look at the structure of the poem. How are the stanzas similar?
b What repetition can you see in the words, **rhymes** and **rhythm** of the poem?
c What sort of images are created in the reader's mind?
d What is the overall mood and message of the poem?
e Who do you think might be the intended audience for this poem? Think about what sort of people Landon may have wanted to influence.

Key terms

rhyme using the same sound to end words, particularly at the ends of lines

rhythm the pattern of beats in a line of music or poetry

Stretch yourself

Write a paragraph to explain how the poet has conveyed a powerful message to the reader in this poem.

1.2: What is a poem?

🧩 Putting it all together

In this unit you have learned that poems, like any text, are written for a purpose, for an audience and usually (although not always) in the form of stanzas. You can recognise poetry by its patterns of language, sound and imagery. These patterns vary from poem to poem. Not all poems have the same features, but they all aim to create powerful images in the reader's mind.

Activity 6

Now you are going to write a poem of your own, using the form of Shukria Rezaei's poem as a guide. Include four short stanzas, with three or four lines in each, and a final line on its own at the end.

Follow the steps below.

Step 1: Discuss your ideas for a poem. Think about describing a time or a place or an event that is special to you and which you remember very clearly.

Step 2: Think about the overall mood you want to convey in your poem to your audience. Is it happy, thoughtful or exciting?

Step 3: Start planning key words, descriptions and comparisons for your poem. You could draw your plan as a spider diagram like this:

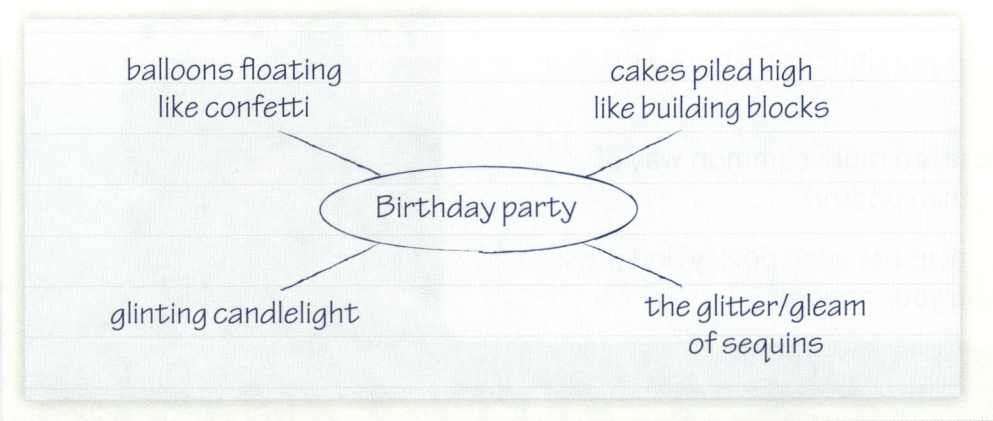

> balloons floating
> like confetti
>
> cakes piled high
> like building blocks
>
> Birthday party
>
> glinting candlelight
>
> the glitter/gleam
> of sequins

Step 4: Try to think of words and images that appeal to different senses, e.g. what you can see/hear/taste/smell/feel.

Step 5: Using the same form as 'I Want a Poem', start writing your poem. If one idea, image or word doesn't work, try another. Make sure the final line is simple but powerful, like a punchline, to make it memorable.

1.3 What's the story?

1: Texts all around us

In this unit, you will:
- learn to recognise prose and understand its different forms
- explore some of the language and features used in prose
- compare different types of stories written in prose.

What's the big idea?
Most texts we read in detail are written in prose. Prose usually means writing in sentences and paragraphs in a way that is similar to how we speak. It is the type of writing that is used for writing narrative texts such as novels, newspaper articles, letters and textbooks like this one.

People have been using prose to tell stories for many centuries. Stories are powerful things. Each story is written or told for a purpose and with an audience in mind. In this unit you will see how writers make different choices depending on their audience and purpose.

Activity 1

a What types of texts can you think of that are written in prose?

b Why do you think prose is a more common way of speaking and writing than poetry?

c What are three differences between poetry and prose? Give reasons to explain your answer.

1.3: What's the story?

Read the text below carefully. Look for the clues about the writer, the form, the audience and the purpose of the text. Refer back to page 12 of unit 1 as a reminder of what audience, purpose and form are.

Nine and seven-year-old brothers are discovered alive after going missing in the Amazon rainforest

After a four week search, young brothers, Glauco and Gleison Ferreira, have miraculously been found alive.

On February 18th, Glauco, seven, and Gleison, nine, set out from home in the **Lago Capanã** nature reserve in search of small birds. When the boys did not return, authorities began a search across the whole of the rainforest in the northwest of Brazil. However, the search was unsuccessful and was called off eight days later.

On Tuesday night, incredibly the brothers were found by a woodcutter when he heard a scream. He discovered the boys four miles away from home, scared of the noise from his chainsaw.

The woodcutter followed the sound and found the brothers lying on the ground, hungry and painfully underweight, with cuts and bruises all over. Once reunited with their parents, they informed them that over the four weeks they had had no access to food and only drank rainwater.

The brothers were taken immediately to hospital in **Manicoré** to be treated for their injuries, malnutrition and dehydration.

Many people gathered to see Glauco and Gleison reunited with their family.

Lago Capanã, Manicoré – places in Brazil

Activity 2

a Where would you expect to read a text like this? Think carefully about the clues that show what type of text this is.

b Who do you think the audience for this text might be?

c What do you think is the writer's purpose in telling this story?

d Do you think it's a true story or is it fiction? Discuss your reasons.

e How involved do you think the writer was in the events that took place?

1: Texts all around us

⭐ Boosting your vocabulary

Writers choose their words carefully. The activity below focuses on some key vocabulary in the source text, highlighted on page 25.

Activity 3

a Look again at the three **adverbs** highlighted in the source text on page 25. How do these adverbs add more drama and detail to the sentences? Think about the impact of the sentences without the adverbs.

b These adverbs are related to the **adjectives** 'miraculous', 'painful' and 'incredible'. Write adverbs relating to each of the following adjectives.

   vicious   playful   humble

c Write three sentences, one for each adverb, showing you understand its meaning.

> ✅ **Tip**
>
> Remember that if the adjective ends in 'e', take it off before adding 'ly'. For example, 'incredible' becomes 'incredibly'.

> 🗝 **Key terms**
>
> **adjective** a word that describes a noun
>
> **adverb** a word that you use with a verb, adjective or other adverb that tells you how, when or where something happened

💡 Building your knowledge

You have learned that some news articles are examples of stories told in prose. The audience for internet news articles can be huge because people have access to read them on a regular basis.

As with all texts, it is important to also think about these features when reading a prose text:

- What is the purpose?
- Is it fact or fiction?
- How does the writer present the story and why?

The three activities that follow will help you to explore these questions in more detail.

> ✅ **Tip**
>
> Writers often have more than one purpose in writing a text. Think about how the writer uses language to add drama and detail to the text, as well as explaining the facts.

Activity 4

Look back at page 13 at the different reasons why people write texts. What do you think was the purpose of writing this news article? Explain your answer.

1.3: What's the story?

Activity 5

Prose texts can be fiction or non-fiction. Stories can be imaginary or true.

In Activity 2, you decided whether the article on page 25 was a true story or fiction. What evidence from the text helped you decide whether it is fiction or non-fiction and what effect does this have on the reader? For example:

> Gives full names and ages of boys – makes the reader believe they are real people, not characters.

When writers tell stories, they can tell the story from a personal point of view as if involved in the events. For example, if the writer tells the story from a personal perspective they might write:

> I was deep in the rainforest, using my chainsaw to cut down a huge tree, when I heard a child crying…

This is called a **first-person narrative.**

In other stories, the writer may tell the story as someone not involved in the events, and they write about it using a **third-person narrative**:

> The boys were found on Tuesday night almost four miles away from home by a tree cutter…

Activity 6

What do you think are the differences between using first- and third-person perspectives? Think about how *reliable* the story is, how *exciting* it is, or how *realistic* it is.

Key terms

first-person narrative a story told by someone as if they were involved in the events themselves, using first-person pronouns, e.g. *I* and *we*

third-person narrative a story told by someone who was not involved in the events themselves, using third-person pronouns, e.g. *he, she, they*

1: Texts all around us

The following extract is from a different type of prose text: a novel.

Extract from *Pigeon English* by Stephen Kelman

You can only see the car park and the bins from my balcony. You can't see the river because the trees are in the way. You can see more and more houses. Lines and lines of them all everywhere like a hell of snakes and smaller flats where the old people live […]

5 I put my coat on and got some flour. It was very late. The helicopters were out looking for robbers again, I could hear them far away. The cold wind bit into my bones like a crazy dog. The trees behind the towers were blowing but the river was asleep…

I love living on floor 9, you can look down and as long as you don't stick out too far nobody on the ground even knows you're there. I was going to do a spit but then I saw somebody by the bins so I swallowed it back up again. He was kneeling on the floor
10 by the bottle bank. He was poking his hand under like he dropped something there. I couldn't see his face because his hood was up.

Me: 'Maybe it's the robber! Quick, helicopter, here's your man! Shine your torchlight down there!' (I only said it inside my head.)

He pulled something from under the bin. It was all wrapped up. He looked all around
15 and then he unwrapped the wrapping.

From this text, you can **infer** that the **narrator** is a child because they say it is getting 'very late' and they assume a helicopter would be looking out for robbers. The text also says they were going to 'do a spit' over the balcony, which is a childish thing to do.

Activity 7

Explain what you can infer about the narrator from the **quotations** below. Look for clues in the text and imagine why and how the narrator could be experiencing these things.

> 'You can only see the car park and the bins from my balcony.'

> '(I only said it inside my head.)'

🔑 Key terms

infer to work something out from what is seen, said or done, even though it is not stated directly

narrator a person who tells a story, especially in a book, play or film

⬆ Stretch yourself

Write a paragraph to explain what we learn about the character of the narrator, using the quotations to help you. You could begin with 'These words suggest that…'

1.3: What's the story?

The author uses language features to bring alive the character of the narrator. For example, he uses a simile to describe the feel of the wind as biting into his bones like a dog.

> Comparing the wind to a crazy dog suggests that the wind was vicious, brutal and sharp like a dog attacking you with its teeth. It makes the narrator sound as if he might be scared of dogs, especially if they are unpredictable.

✓ **Tip**

When analysing language features, such as similies, think about how it makes you feel or what it makes you picture, to identify what impact the author is trying to create.

Activity 8

The author uses a simile in lines 2–3 to describe the houses: 'Lines and lines of them all everywhere like a hell of snakes'. Explain what this could suggest about the narrator's view of the houses and his life experiences.

🔑 **Key term**

quotation a word or phrase from a text

🧩 Putting it all together

Activity 9

a   Compare the two prose texts by completing a chart like the one below to identify the different features of the texts. Choose the features which you think are most appropriate.

'Nine and seven-year-old brothers are discovered'	Pigeon English

factual language   descriptive language   to entertain   to inform   to instruct   to advise

to persuade   fiction   non-fiction   real life   imaginary   first-person narrative

third-person narrative   general audience   audience of young people   sequence of events

✏ b   Write three sentences to compare the two prose texts. Include the features in the table above in your answer. You could also include words such as 'whereas', 'similarly', 'unlike' or 'both' to link your ideas together.

1: Texts all around us

1.4 Why all the drama?

In this unit, you will:
- learn to identify the key features of drama texts
- explore and compare two forms of drama
- create, perform and record your own piece of drama.

What's the big idea?

People across the world have been creating, writing and performing drama for thousands of years. The earliest dramas were performed live by actors in front of an audience, but nowadays, dramas can be pre-recorded. Drama can be experienced in different ways, such as listening to a play or watching one on television.

Drama is central to our everyday lives. From pantomimes to podcasts, street performances to soap operas and blockbusters, we are surrounded by drama. But have you ever thought about the people who write, or script, these dramas? What makes a drama a drama? Who are dramas written for and what is their purpose? This unit will help you to answer these questions.

Key term

character a person in a drama or story

Activity 1

Discuss your favourite dramas to watch or listen to.

a Who do you think they were written for, and why?

b How many different places can you think of where you can watch or listen to drama?

c What do you think makes a drama text different from a short story or poem?

About 500 years ago, William Shakespeare was a successful playwright. His plays are still popular today because they deal with elaborate **characters**, relationships and situations, and include themes, such as love, power, jealousy and ambition, which audiences can identify with.

1.4: Why all the drama?

The extract below is from Shakespeare's play *Romeo and Juliet*. In this extract, 13-year-old Juliet Capulet has just fallen in love with a stranger at a party at her house. As the guests leave, she asks the Nurse, who has brought her up, to tell her who each of the guests is in order to find out the stranger's name.

> **Key term**
>
> **stage direction** an instruction to an actor about movement or expression, or a description of a sound effect

Extract from *Romeo and Juliet* by William Shakespeare

Exeunt all but Juliet and Nurse

Juliet	Come **hither**, Nurse. What is **yond** gentleman?
Nurse	The son and heir of old Tiberio.
Juliet	What's he that now is going out of door?
Nurse	**Marry**, that I think be young Petruchio.
Juliet	What's he that follows there, that would not dance?
Nurse	I know not.
Juliet	Go ask his name.—If he be married,
	My grave is like to be my wedding bed.
Nurse	His name is Romeo, and a Montague,
	The only son of your great enemy.
Juliet	My only love sprung from my only hate!
	Too early seen unknown, and known too late!
	Prodigious birth of love it is to me,
	That I must love a loathed enemy.
Nurse	What's tis? what's tis?
Juliet	A rhyme I learnt even now
	Of one I danc'd **withal**.

One calls within 'Juliet!'

Nurse	**Anon**, anon!
	Come, let's away, the strangers all are gone.

Exeunt

---

exeunt – a stage direction meaning characters leave the stage
hither – here
yond – that … over there
marry – (at the start of a sentence) well, indeed
withal – with
anon – coming or soon

The name of the character indicates who speaks the words that follow.

Like her father, Juliet is a Capulet and they have a feud with the Montague family.

The italic font indicates a **stage direction**, telling actors what to do, or sound effects, as here.

31

1: Texts all around us

⭐ Boosting your vocabulary

Writers choose their words carefully. The activity below focuses on some vocabulary from the source text, highlighted on page 31.

Activity 2

a   The Nurse uses the word 'heir' to describe one of the young men at the party. An heir is someone who inherits money or property from someone in their family. Why do you think the Nurse might comment to Juliet that this young man is an 'heir'?

b   Juliet uses the word 'loathed' to describe her family's enemies, the Montagues. Write down three words which mean the same as 'loathe' and at least three words which mean the opposite.

c   The word 'prodigious' has two meanings. It can mean huge and immense or it can mean problematic. Which of these meanings fits best with Juliet's words in lines 14–15?

> ✅ **Tip**
>
> Juliet is only 13 years old but her parents are keen to find her a husband. This would have been common at the time, but would be considered a human rights issue today.

Activity 3

a   Write a short script on a similar theme in modern English. Use the same structure to lay out your script as the extract on page 31 does.

b   With a partner, practise reading your modern script aloud.

💡 Building your knowledge

A drama text is called a script and is based on **dialogue** between characters. Sometimes characters have a **monologue**, expressing their thoughts aloud, giving the audience an insight into their ideas and feelings.

Most dramas tell a story. These stories may be based on real or imaginary events. After the **setting** is established, the characters meet a problem or engage in a **conflict**. The action then rises to a **climax**, which usually resolves the conflict by the end of the play.

The purposes of a play can vary. Plays are nearly always written to entertain people, but many also carry a message or draw attention to an issue.

> 🔑 **Key terms**
>
> **climax** when the action is at its most exciting or interesting
>
> **conflict** a struggle or disagreement between people
>
> **dialogue** words spoken by characters
>
> **monologue** a speech by one character
>
> **setting** where the action takes place

1.4: Why all the drama?

Activity 4

In a play, the writer has to portray the characters through the words they speak. It is up to the audience to infer details about the characters. In the *Romeo and Juliet* extract, the Nurse doesn't say much, but we learn a lot about her character from the dialogue.

a   Find a line of dialogue to support each of these inferences about the Nurse's character:
   i   She knows a lot of people.
   ii   She's interested in people's money.
   iii She's nosy and wants to know Juliet's business.
   iv   She's quick to respond to instructions.

b   Now let's focus on Juliet. What do you understand about Juliet's character from the lines of dialogue below? The first one has been done for you.
   i   "What's he that now is going out of door?"

> Juliet asks the Nurse about two other young men before she asks about Romeo, which suggests that she is secretive, trying to hide who she is really interested in.

   ii   "Go ask his name."
   iii "If he be married, / My grave is like to be my wedding bed."
   iv   "My only love sprung from my only hate!"

Activity 5

a   Which dramatic themes do you think Shakespeare introduces in this extract?

b   Why do you think a writer might choose to write a drama text, rather than a short story or poem? What does drama offer that the other forms don't?

1: Texts all around us

For centuries, drama was only performed on stage. With the arrival of radio, film and television, drama took on a new life. The drama script below was written to be listened to as a podcast. In this science fiction drama, 'Here Be Dragons', four scientists have been tasked by the government to investigate a new breed of sea monster. We meet the characters here aboard their submarine, far beneath the ocean.

Extract from an episode of 'Here Be Dragons' by Jordan Cobb

*The crew is gathered together in **Ops**. Scarlett is standing over Harper's shoulder, studying the navigational display.*

Scarlett Check it again.

Harper Commander-

5 Scarlett Check. The charts. Again.

Harper (sighs) Running navigational software and sonar sweep... Again.

We hear her typing, flicking a few switches.

Harper (cont'd) ... **Sonar** is still nonfunctional. (under her breath) No surprise there. (louder) And analogue record of our coordinates is the same.

10 Scarlett Officer Campbell, what's the status on that diagnostic?

Pip Ship's computer system is running normally, commander. **Ophelia's** run three self checks, and I've done two manually. There's no problem with the **Rusalka's** hardware or software.

Scarlett There HAS to be. Look at these coordinates! Look. Right now, we should be here. See? There should be islands, here, and here. Somewhere to stock up on supplies, refuel. But

15 you look out the window? Nothing. Just open ocean. We're approximately 390,000 square miles further south than we should be. Which means we've been running off course for... days. Maybe weeks. And Ophelia hasn't caught it. (beat. for once, not in a rage) It has to be a problem with engineering. I need you to tell me what you did.

Pip I...

20 Atlas Pip didn't do anything. I did.

Pip Dr. Atlas-

Atlas It's alright. (turning to Scarlett) ... I've been making adjustments to the heading for the past few weeks. Every night on the Graveyard Shift. beat.

Scarlett ...You? ...What?

25 *BOOM! The whole ship shakes and there is a crunching, scraping sound as the bottom of the hull hits something.*

Atlas Is everyone okay?!

There is a general groan of ascent as the crew pushes themselves up from the floor.

Harper What on Earth was that? Did we hit something?

Ops – the operation room
sonar – a technique that uses sound waves to see underwater
Ophelia – the original name of the submarine when it was used and sunk in World War 2
Rusalka – the new name of the submarine now it has been renovated

1.4: Why all the drama?

Activity 6

In this unit, you have read two different drama texts. Complete the spider diagram opposite, adding the key features of a drama text that you have identified. Think about the features of scripts as well as the performance and storyline.

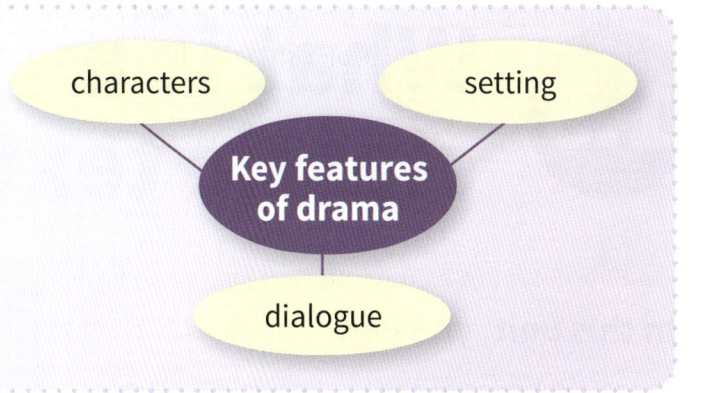

Key features of drama: characters, setting, dialogue

Putting it all together

Activity 7

Write your own short audio drama script to perform and review in small groups. Follow the steps below.

Step 1: Think about the purpose of your drama. What point are you trying to get across?

Step 2: Who is your target audience? Who will watch your drama?

Step 3: Think about the setting for your drama. Where will it take place?

Step 4: Think about your characters. Do they know each other as family or friends or are they strangers? Make sure each person has a character to play.

Step 5: What will happen in your drama? It has to be short but dramatic, so consider what the climax of your drama will be – does someone get injured, or find out terrible news, or is there a happy ending?

Step 6: Now write the script. Add any sound effects or stage directions that you think will improve the drama, but remember that the dialogue is the most important feature.

Step 7: When the script is complete, read it through several times to make sure you are all familiar with the words. Then perform and record the podcast.

> **Tip**
>
> Remember to look back at the diagram you completed in Activity 6 to remind you of the key features of drama as you write your script.

1: Texts all around us

1.5 What is a classic text?

In this unit, you will:
- learn what qualities make a text a classic
- explore how language and structural features are used to help to build character
- write about a classic text, showing your understanding of its appeal.

What's the big idea?
Have you ever wondered why we continue to read and study some texts hundreds of years after they've been written? A classic text is one that is remembered in history and considered worth reading or studying because of its literary quality and authorship. But what makes a text a 'classic' and who decides?

Classic texts can be novels, poems or drama scripts. They differ in their themes and **genres** but often share similar qualities. Many classic texts are based on adventures; some are based on an imaginary world created by the writer, while some offer ideas about what is good and evil.

Activity 1

a List some classic texts for children that you have heard of or read.

b What do you think makes a classic text?

c Which books that are popular now do you think will still be popular in 100 years' time and why? For example, is the *Harry Potter* series a classic for future generations?

Key terms

fantasy an imaginary story that is not based on reality

genre a type of story, e.g. *horror, romance, adventure, science fiction*

mythical from a myth, a traditional story that often includes supernatural beings

In this unit, we will look at an example of a traditional children's classic, *The Lion, the Witch and the Wardrobe* by C.S. Lewis. Historically, most classic texts were written by a relatively privileged group of white, male authors, who often had a higher status and better access to education than other authors. However, as society changes, a more diverse range of author voices are being heard and published, bringing new ideas expressed in original ways.

1.5: What is a classic text?

In the story, a young girl named Lucy is playing hide and seek with her siblings. She climbs through the back of a wardrobe, into a **fantasy** world of talking creatures and eternal winter.

In this extract, Lucy has just arrived and meets a Faun, a **mythical** creature that is half man and half goat. While you are reading, think about what you know about the story and why it might be a classic.

Extract from *The Lion, the Witch and the Wardrobe* by C.S. Lewis

"Good evening," said Lucy. But the Faun was so busy picking up its parcels that at first it did not reply. When it had finished it made her a little bow.

5 "Good evening, good evening," said the Faun. "Excuse me – I don't want to be inquisitive – but should I be right in thinking that you are a **Daughter of Eve**?"

"My name's Lucy," said she, not quite
10 understanding him.

"But you are – forgive me – you are what they call a girl?" asked the Faun.

"Of course I'm a girl," said Lucy.

"You are in fact Human?"

15 "Of course I'm human," said Lucy, still a little puzzled.

"To be sure, to be sure," said the Faun. "How stupid of me! But I've never seen a **Son of Adam** or a Daughter of Eve before. I am delighted.
20 That is to say –" and then it stopped as if it had been going to say something it had not intended but had remembered in time. "Delighted, delighted," it went on. "Allow me to introduce myself. My name is Tumnus."

25 "I am very pleased to meet you, Mr Tumnus," said Lucy.

"And may I ask, O Lucy Daughter of Eve," said Mr Tumnus, "how you have come into Narnia?"

"Narnia? What's that?" said Lucy.

30 "This is the land of Narnia," said the Faun, "where we are now; all that lies between the lamp-post and the great castle of Cair Paravel on the eastern sea. And you – you have come from the wild woods of the west?"

35 "I – I got in through the wardrobe in the spare room," said Lucy.

"Ah!" said Mr Tumnus in a rather melancholy voice, "if only I had worked harder at geography when I was a little Faun, I should no
40 doubt know all about those strange countries. It is too late now."

"But they aren't countries at all," said Lucy, almost laughing. "It's only just back there – at least – I'm not sure. It is summer there."

45 "Meanwhile," said Mr Tumnus, "it is winter in Narnia, and has been for ever so long, and we shall both catch cold if we stand here talking in the snow. Daughter of Eve from the far land of Spare Oom where eternal summer reigns
50 around the bright city of War Drobe, how would it be if you came and had tea with me?"

"Thank you very much, Mr Tumnus," said Lucy. "But I was wondering whether I ought to be getting back."

45 "It's only just round the corner," said the Faun, "and there'll be a roaring fire – and toast – and sardines – and cake."

"Well, it's very kind of you," said Lucy. "But I shan't be able to stay long."

Daughter of Eve, Son of Adam – in the Christian story of creation, Eve and Adam were the first woman and man that God created and are considered the ancestors of all other humans

1: Texts all around us

⭐ Boosting your vocabulary

Writers choose their words carefully. The activity below focuses on some key vocabulary in the source text, which has been highlighted on page 37.

Activity 2

a 'Inquisitive' means curious. What other adjectives could the writer have used in the second paragraph to describe the Faun's attitude?

b The word 'ought' is an example of a **modal verb**. Identify the modal verb in each of the following sentences. Then use a different modal verb in each sentence to see how it changes the meaning.

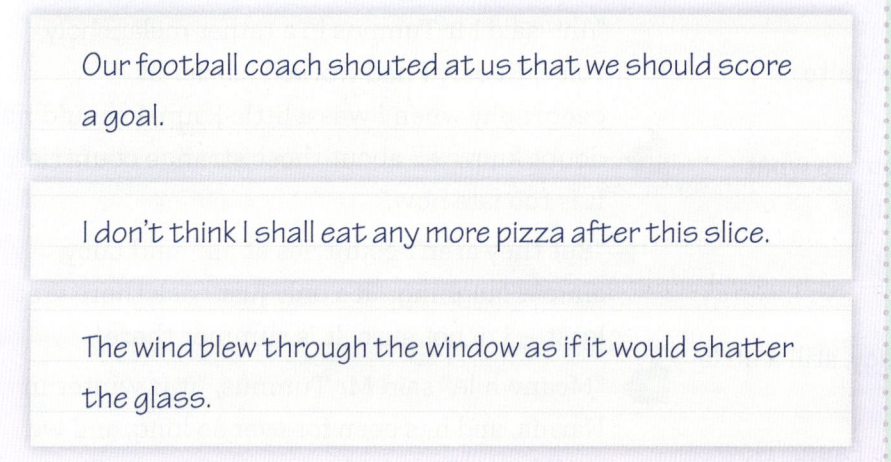

> Our football coach shouted at us that we should score a goal.

> I don't think I shall eat any more pizza after this slice.

> The wind blew through the window as if it would shatter the glass.

c The writer describes the Faun as 'melancholy', which means he is sad and thoughtful. Rank these words in order of how intense the feeling of sadness is.

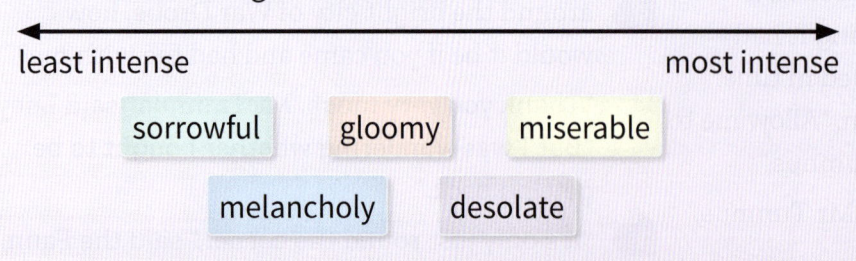

←——————————————————→
least intense   most intense

sorrowful   gloomy   miserable

melancholy   desolate

d The word 'reigns' means rules or dominates. Read the list of words below out loud. What do all these words have in common?

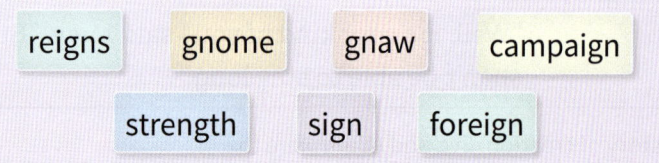

reigns   gnome   gnaw   campaign

strength   sign   foreign

🔑 Key term

modal verb a verb that works with another verb to show that something needs to happen or might possibly happen, e.g. *must, shall, will, should, would, can, could, may* and *might*

✅ Tip

Not all modal verbs will work in every sentence. Keep trying them out until you find one that makes sense.

1.5: What is a classic text?

Building your knowledge

Classic texts often share similar qualities, which could be:

- a universal appeal to readers
- strong, memorable characters
- high entertainment value
- a powerful message
- a unique point of view
- an outstanding quality of writing.

The Lion, the Witch and the Wardrobe is an example of a text that includes all of these qualities.

Activity 3

a Read the list of key elements in the story of *The Lion, the Witch and the Wardrobe* below. Where have you seen these elements in other films, books or television series?

- A child goes on an adventure alone.
- The child discovers a fantasy world beyond the real world.
- The child meets unusual fantasy characters.
- The child triggers change in a magical world.
- The child faces challenges but ultimately succeeds.
- There is a battle between good and evil.

b Why do you think these elements are so common in stories? Do you agree that they have timeless appeal?

Writers use language and **structural features** to create strong and memorable characters and to give the reader insights into their thoughts and feelings. In the extract from *The Lion, the Witch and the Wardrobe*, the text focuses on Lucy's perspective and her thoughts about the Faun. This means the reader is more likely to identify with Lucy's character and relate to how she feels puzzled when the Faun asks her if she is a girl and a human.

The author also uses dialogue to *show* us what the characters are like, rather than simply *telling* us. The reader doesn't know what the Faun is thinking, but we can infer traits of his character and how he feels from what he says. We can tell the Faun is anxious through the repetition in his speech: 'you are… you are what they call a girl?' This shows he is nervous when he first meets Lucy, probably because he has never met a human before.

Key term

structural feature a feature used by a writer to give a text its overall shape

39

1: Texts all around us

When you read a text closely, you can see the quality of the writing. You can understand how the writer has used language and structural features to create particular effects.

Activity 4

Match the feature on the left with the effect on the reader on the right. Think about what the writer might be trying to achieve.

Feature	Effect
The writer focuses mainly on Lucy's thoughts and perspective	to show the contrast between different characters' views.
The writer uses capital letters in the Faun's speech that describes Lucy	to show that they are both nervous and eager to please.
The writer uses lots of dialogue in the text	to show that the Faun thinks Lucy is interesting and important.
The writer uses repetition in the Faun and Lucy's dialogue	to give the reader an insight into Lucy's feelings.

When you write about texts to analyse the writing, you need to provide evidence for your comments by selecting examples or quotations from the text itself.

Activity 5

Find a quotation to support each of the features and effects in Activity 4. For example, a quotation from the text to support the first feature and effect could be the below.

The writer focuses mainly on Lucy's thoughts and perspective → A quotation that shows this would be 'still a little puzzled'.

40

1.5: What is a classic text?

Putting it all together

Activity 6

Now let's look at a reading question that needs a longer answer.

> How does the writer give the reader an insight into the characters in this extract from *The Lion, the Witch and the Wardrobe*?

To answer the question, you need to combine the feature, the effect and the supporting quotation to make a point, like in the example below.

> In *The Lion, the Witch and the Wardrobe*, the writer has given the reader an insight into the characters by using lots of different features. One feature the writer uses is to show us what happens from Lucy's perspective, not the Faun's. An example of this is when the Faun meets Lucy and asks if she is a Daughter of Eve. In the text it says Lucy is 'still a little puzzled'. The effect of the writer doing this is to encourage the reader to share Lucy's thoughts and feelings. When the reader hears what Lucy's thoughts and feelings are, they realise how confused she is and this creates a sense of strangeness and fantasy. It also makes the reader identify with Lucy and care what happens to her.

- Introduction
- Feature
- Example/Quotation
- Effect
- Explanation linked to the question

✏️ Using the example above as a model, write a paragraph about each of the other features in Activity 4. You should include the feature, a quotation, the effect and an explanation of how the effect links to the question.

❓ Did you know?

C.S. Lewis wrote seven books about Narnia. In every story he introduced new characters as well as expanding on the stories of characters from previous books. *The Chronicles of Narnia* have been popular since they were written in the 1950s.

1: Texts all around us

1.6 How is your voice heard?

In this unit, you will:
- learn how to share your views effectively
- explore the context, style and features of a powerful speech
- write and present a short speech to express your point of view.

What's the big idea?
As you learned in the previous unit, classic texts have qualities that can appeal to readers in a timeless way. In this unit, one writer talks about how, as a child, she loved reading classic texts, even though they were rooted in times and places that were unfamiliar to her. She highlights the need for children to discover stories and writers from a range of different backgrounds and experiences, so they realise that books can tell many stories, rather than a single one.

The Internet has brought opportunities for people to communicate more widely and more easily than ever before. Writers and speakers can now reach a global audience of billions. Does this mean books and newspaper texts are no longer important? How can you get your voice heard above everyone else's?

Activity 1

a Which do you think is the most powerful way to express ideas?

b Where do you find most of the texts you read?

c Speeches can be listened to in person, watched online or read through a **transcript**. How do you access speeches and how often?

d How do you think the way you access a speech affects how you understand the message the speaker is trying to get across? Explain your answer.

Key term
transcript a written record of spoken words

Did you know?
TED stands for Technology Entertainment Design. The TED Talks began in 1984 with the purpose of 'spreading ideas'. There are currently more than 3500 TED talks available online, which have been accessed over a billion times. That's a big audience!

Read the text opposite, which is taken from a speech given by the writer Chimamanda Ngozi Adichie in 2009 as part of a series of speeches called TED Talks. As well as the original live audience, the speech has had over 30 million views on the Internet.

Extract from 'The Danger of a Single Story', a TED Talk by Chimamanda Ngozi Adichie

I'm a storyteller. And I would like to tell you a few personal stories about what I like to call 'the danger of the single story'. I grew up on a university campus in eastern Nigeria. My mother says that I started reading at the age of two, although I think four is probably close to the truth. So I was an early reader, and what I read were British and American children's books.

I was also an early writer, and when I began to write, at about the age of seven, stories in pencil with crayon illustrations that my poor mother was obligated to read, I wrote exactly the kinds of stories I was reading. All my characters were white and blue-eyed. They played in the snow. They ate apples. And they talked a lot about the weather, how lovely it was that the sun had come out. Now, this despite the fact that I lived in Nigeria. I had never been outside Nigeria. We didn't have snow. We ate mangoes. And we never talked about the weather, because there was no need to. [...]

What this demonstrates, I think, is how impressionable and vulnerable we are in the face of a story, particularly as children. Because all I had read were books in which characters were foreign. I had become convinced that books by their very nature had to have foreigners in them and had to be about things with which I could not personally identify. Now, things changed when I discovered African books. There weren't many of them available and they weren't quite as easy to find as the foreign books.

But because of writers like **Chinua Achebe** and **Camara Laye**, I went through a mental shift in my **perception** of literature. I realized that people like me, girls with skin the color of chocolate, whose kinky hair could not form ponytails, could also exist in literature. I started to write about things I recognized.

Now, I loved those American and British books I read. They stirred my imagination. They opened up new worlds for me. But the **unintended consequence** was that I did not know that people like me could exist in literature. So what the discovery of African writers did for me was this: it saved me from having a single story of what books are.

Chinua Achebe – well-known Nigerian writer
Camara Laye – well-known Guinean writer

perception – view or understanding of something
unintended consequence – unplanned result

1: Texts all around us

⭐ Boosting your vocabulary

Writers choose their words carefully. The activity below focuses on some key vocabulary in the source text, which has been highlighted on page 43.

> 🔑 **Key term**
>
> **antonym** a word that has the opposite meaning of a particular word

Activity 2

a The word 'campus' in the extract may be unfamiliar to you. However, there are clues in the text to work out what it means.
  i 'I grew up on a university campus.' Does this suggest that a campus is a place or a person?
  ii A university is a college for older students. Do you think it's bigger or smaller than a school?
  iii What does the word 'camp' in 'campus' make you think of?

b The writer describes young readers as 'impressionable' and 'vulnerable'. Look at how the word 'impressionable' is explored in the Frayer model below.

Frayer model

Definition
easily influenced or affected by someone else

Characteristics
- adjective
- linked to the verb 'to impress', which means to fix an idea firmly into the mind or literally to press a mark into something
- from an old French word *presser*, meaning 'to press'

Word
impressionable

Examples
- The boy was impressionable, so would often copy his friends.
- The sand on the beach was damp and impressionable, so we drew patterns.

Antonyms
- resilient
- hard
- strong
- solid

Create your own Frayer model diagram to explore the word 'vulnerable'. Use the same four headings: definition, characteristics, examples and antonyms.

1.6: How is your voice heard?

Building your knowledge

When and where we grow up, and the influences around us, are the **context** we experience as readers. Context affects the way we read, understand and respond to texts. Context is important for writers too. Adichie wrote this speech as a Nigerian writer in the 21st century.

Activity 3

a   Describe the context when Adichie first began to read as a child.

b   What effect did this have when she started to write her own stories?

c   What did Adichie realise when she first read stories by African writers?

The **tone** of a spoken or written text describes how the writer feels about their subject and how they want the reader to feel. It is one of the key features of a speech.

Activity 4

a   Choose three adjectives from the panels below which you think best describe the writer's tone in the extract from Adichie's speech. Explain your choices.

calm   excited   serious   humorous

embarrassed   frustrated   angry   surprised

b   Read the speech aloud using a different tone. You could try reading it in an angry, gentle or enthusiastic way. What impact do you think the tone of the speech has on the listener?

c   Other features used by writers in speeches include:
- short sentences for impact
- paragraphs/pauses to change topic
- first-person narrative and **anecdotes**
- informal language
- repetition of key phrases or ideas.

Find an example of each of these features in Adichie's speech.

Stretch yourself

Summarise the ways that your knowledge of books, writers and your personal experiences could affect your understanding and how you respond to different texts.

Key terms

anecdote a short or entertaining story about real people or events

context the time, place and influences on a text from when it was written, and from when it is read, which shape our understanding of the text

tone the writer's feeling or attitude expressed towards their subject

45

1: Texts all around us

Activity 5

In the extract, Adichie talks about her childhood and the types of stories she read and wrote. But what is her overall view?

a Discuss the following statements.

> All children's books should have characters with a range of lived experiences.

> Writers should only write stories about people and places from their own experience.

> Your sense of identity can be affected by the books you read.

> Children should only read books about children who are like them.

b Identify any statements above that you don't agree with. Change them so that you agree with them.

Activity 6

Which statements did you change in Activity 5 and why?

Present your point of view to your group. Make sure you:

- use a range of words to express your views effectively
- keep your focus on the task
- organise what you say about the two statements clearly.

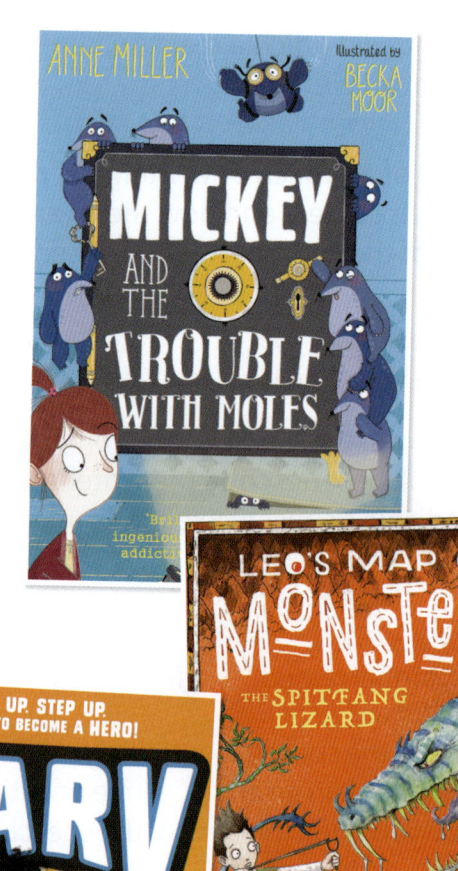

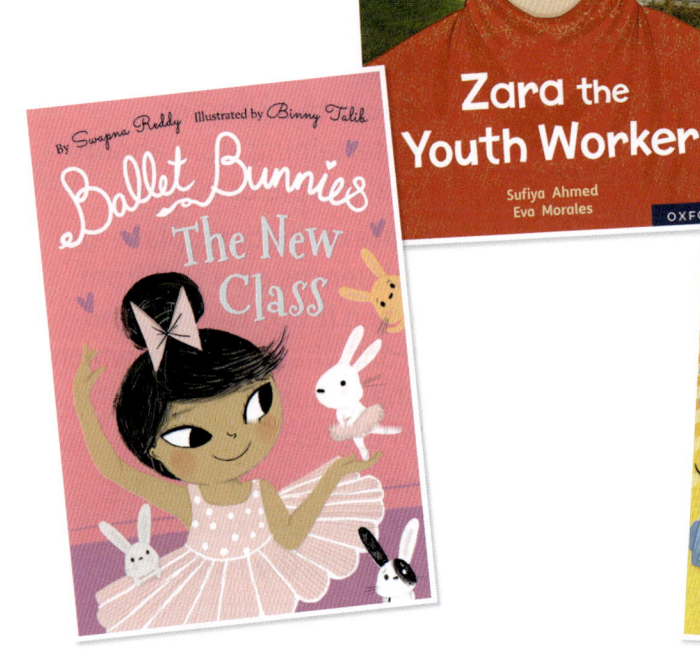

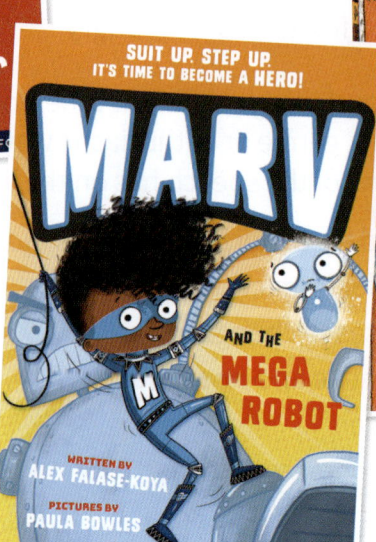

1.6: How is your voice heard?

Putting it all together

Activity 7

In her speech, Adichie talks about a subject she feels passionate about. Now you are going to write a speech about a subject you feel strongly about. It could be about:
- sport
- music
- parents
- social media
- climate
- anything else you feel strongly about.

Once you have an idea, follow the steps below. (One student's ideas are given as an example.)

Step 1: Summarise your point of view in one sentence.
Parents these days are too protective of their children and don't give them enough freedom.

Step 2: Plan three points you will make to support and explain your point of view.
Parents are too scared by news stories about bad things happening to let their children play outside…

Step 3: Start your speech by writing your summary sentence and explaining the context in which you are writing.
Parents these days are too protective of their children and don't give them enough freedom. I'm 12 years old and I think my parents protect me too much..

Step 4: Write three paragraphs – one for each point you want to make, adding as much detail and evidence as you can.
There are news stories every day about bad things happening in the world. I believe this makes parents more scared and…

Step 5: Finish your speech by reinforcing your overall point of view.

Activity 8

Now present your speech to the class. Take time to rehearse so you feel more confident.

Remember to:
- express your attitude through your tone of voice
- use your hands and facial expressions to emphasise your feelings.

> ✓ **Tip**
>
> Try to use some of the features of speeches that you explored in Activity 4 in your own speech.

47

1: Texts all around us

1.7 Which English do you speak?

In this unit, you will:
- learn how texts are influenced by a writer's background and the language they use
- explore differences between Standard and non-standard English
- write a drama script, including characters who are code-switching.

What's the big idea?

The language we use when we write texts or speak out loud can say a lot about our purpose and our audience, as well as hinting at our identity and background. Some of us are **bilingual** and may speak to our family in one language and to our friends and teachers in another language. Or if you speak one language, you may speak in a dialect belonging to the area where you live, where you were born, or where your parents were born. You may choose to speak in your own dialect but to write in Standard English. How we decide which language or dialect to use when we speak and write depends on our purpose and audience.

Activity 1

a The way we speak often depends on who we are talking to. How and why do you change the way you speak?

b When you write, how does your language change depending on whether you are sending a text or doing your homework?

c Do you speak another language or **dialect** as well as **Standard English**? How does this link to your sense of who you are?

Did you know?

In the UK, 36% of people speak more than one language fluently – that's 24 million adults and millions more children and young people.

Key terms

bilingual able to speak two languages

dialect a form of a language linked to a specific region, e.g. Geordie in Newcastle upon Tyne

Standard English a widely recognised formal version of English, not linked to any region, but used in schools, exams, official publications and in public announcements

The two texts opposite are both written by Benjamin Zephaniah, a British poet from Birmingham with a Jamaican background. Read them both carefully and look for differences between the texts. Text A was published in a collection of poems for young people; Text B was published online in a national newspaper.

48

1.7: Which English do you speak?

Text A: 'Running' by Benjamin Zephaniah

I reckon I could run de world,
I used to run me school,
Hundred metres an two hundred metres,
I could run up Mount Everest
5 Wid a drink,
I could run tings wid big words
Like,
INFRASTRUCTURE,
an
10 TELECOMMUNICATION,
A marathon? Easy.
I could run out of bounds,
I run wild all de time
I run tings nice ... as dey sey in Jamaica,
15 Or cool ... as dey sey in Iceland,
I could run de Universe ... in verse
But I haven't been given a chance.
I will get my chance,
Politicians are running outta ideas,
20 Dat may mean dat we all, you and me,
I an I,
All of we, may hav to run our own lives,
Dats bad ... as dey sey in New York,
Way out ... as dey sey in space,
25 All right ... as dey sey in
Llanfairpwllgwyngyllgogerychwyrndrobwllllantysiliogogogoch.

Llanfairpwllgwyngyllgogerychwyrndrobwllllantysiliogogogoch – a village in Wales

---

Text B: Extract from an article by Benjamin Zephaniah

I woke up on the morning of November 13 wondering how the government could be overthrown and what could replace it, and then I noticed a letter from the prime minister's
5 office. It said: 'The prime minister has asked me to inform you, in strict confidence, that he has in mind, on the occasion of the forthcoming list of **New Year's honours** to submit your name to the Queen with a recommendation
10 that Her Majesty may be graciously pleased to approve that you be appointed an officer of the **Order of the British Empire**.'

Me? I thought, OBE me? [...] I get angry when I hear that word 'empire'; it reminds me of
15 slavery, it reminds of thousands of years of brutality. [...] It is because of this idea of empire that black people like myself don't even know our true names or our true historical culture. I am not one of those who are obsessed with
20 their roots, and I'm certainly not suffering from a crisis of identity; my obsession is about the future and the political rights of all people. Benjamin Zephaniah OBE – no way **Mr Blair**, no way Mrs Queen. I am profoundly anti-empire.

New Year's honours – the list of people announced every year who will receive a royal honour

Order of the British Empire (OBE) – a royal honour awarded to people for significant achievements
Mr Blair – Tony Blair, UK Prime Minister at that time

1: Texts all around us

⭐ Boosting your vocabulary

Writers choose their words carefully. The activity below focuses on some key vocabulary in the source text, which has been highlighted on page 49.

🔑 Key terms

root the core of a word that has meaning. It may or may not be a complete word

suffix a word or group of letters placed at the end of another word or root to add to or change its meaning

Activity 2

a   Find the words 'graciously' and 'profoundly' in the text. 'Graciously' means something is done politely and kindly. 'Profoundly' means something is done or felt deeply and intensely. Both words are adverbs to explain *how* something is done.

Write two sentences using 'graciously' and 'profoundly' to show you understand their meaning.

b   Many words have a stem or **root** that is added to with **suffixes**. For example, the root *brut* is from the Latin word *brutus*, meaning heavy, dull and stupid. From this root, many more words can be created, such as 'brute' and 'brutal'.

Complete the diagram below by adding as many words as possible that use the same root.

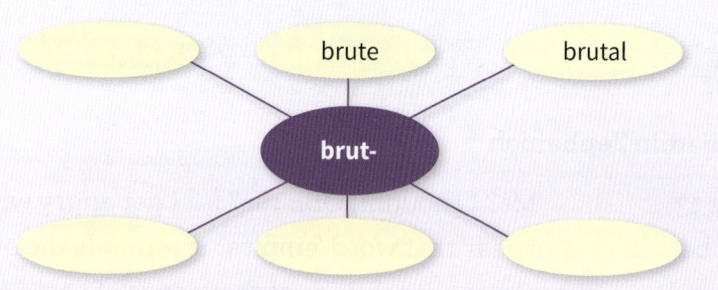

```
         brute        brutal
              \       /
               brut-
              /   |   \
```

c   The 'empire' that Zephaniah refers to is the British Empire, which grew to cover almost a quarter of the globe in the 19th and early 20th centuries. The Empire brought great wealth and power to Britain but not always to the other countries involved. Zephaniah says he is 'anti-empire'. What do you think he means?

d   The word 'obsessed' means your mind is continually filled with the same thought. It comes from the Latin word *obsessus*, meaning haunted or besieged. Like the root 'brut', the root 'obsess' is the basis for many different words.

Write three sentences using a different form of the word 'obsess' in each. For example:

> After the burglary, she checked *obsessively* that her door was locked.

1.7: Which English do you speak?

In the texts on page 49, Benjamin Zephaniah expresses his views on two different subjects. In the poem 'Running', he says he is running out of patience with the country's leaders and he is calling on people to join him in taking control. In the article, Zephaniah explains that he is rejecting the OBE that he has been awarded because it reminds him of a part of Britain's history that he strongly disagrees with.

Activity 3

a Create a list of the differences between the two texts.

Feature	Text A	Text B
Subject		
Form		
Language		
Dialect		
Tone		
Audience		
Purpose		

b Which of the two texts do you think is the most powerful in presenting the writer's point of view? Explain your reasons.

c Why do you think the writer chooses to use very different language in the two texts?

d Why do you think Zephaniah used a different form for the two texts? Think about what impact the poem has in comparison to the newspaper article and who the audiences are.

Activity 4

Zephaniah uses Jamaican dialect in the poem 'Running'. Other people use dialect in their everyday language, depending on where they live. In the West Country, for example, people use dialect words and phrases such as 'keener' and 'gurt lush'.

Find six dialect words or phrases, either included in the poem or from another dialect that is not your own, and explain their meaning. There are some examples to begin with below.

> keener – someone who works hard or is enthusiastic, especially in school
>
> gurt lush – really lovely; 'gurt' means big or great; 'lush' means nice or beautiful

51

1: Texts all around us

Building your knowledge

Benjamin Zephaniah chose to write a poem in his own Jamaican dialect to persuade young people to see the failures of politicians. However, he switched to using more formal language to write a serious article for a more general audience to explain his rejection of an OBE. **Code-switching** is when you move from one language or level of formality to another.

People often switch the language they use, depending on their audience, their purpose and the context of their speech or writing. In a formal context, such as a classroom, or writing for a teacher, you are likely to use formal language and Standard English. In the playground or at home, with your friends or family, speaking or texting, you are more likely to use informal language and **non-standard English**.

Key terms

code-switching moving between different levels of formality in language, e.g. between Standard English and non-standard English

non-standard English an informal version of English, often used with family and friends, including slang and regional variations

Activity 5

a Read the two school reports below.

> (Charlotte has) made limited progress in Science this year. She struggles to listen or concentrate, which is causing significant frustration among her teachers. She needs to make a substantial effort to improve her work and behaviour as soon as possible, or she risks being excluded from the school. Charlotte needs to act now to make a real change in her attitude.

> (Charlie's) done rubbish in Science this year. She doesn't listen to a word I say! I'm fed up with 'er. She needs to crack on with her work and sort 'erself out asap. Or she'll end up getting chucked outta here. Sort it Charlie, now!

b List the differences between the two reports. The first difference has been circled for you.

c Using what you have learned from this activity, compile a list of features that should be included in Standard English and another list of features found in non-standard English.

Stretch yourself

Standard English has been the language of power for many hundreds of years, and other variations, dialects and accents have been considered less serious, less important and having less value. Why do you think one version of English has been seen as more powerful than another?

1.7: Which English do you speak?

You have seen in this unit how important it is to value your own language or dialect, but also how important it is to use Standard English when you need to. Writers and speakers like Benjamin Zephaniah make choices about what language and dialect they use in their texts to engage as wide an audience as possible.

Activity 6

Discuss or write your response to the following statements:
- If people don't like how you speak then it's their problem not yours.
- Some people think that using non-standard English makes you sound less intelligent.
- The way you talk is the real you, and you should always write like that too.

Putting it all together

Activity 7

Now you are going to write a short drama set in the playground at school. There will be two or three student characters and a character who is a teacher, who appears partway through the scene.

Follow the steps below.

Step 1: Decide on your characters and give them names.

Step 2: Plan the scene and what happens. Try to create a conflict between the characters. Will there be a happy ending or will it finish with more conflict?

Step 3: Write your drama. Think carefully about the language the student characters will use. They don't all have to use the same language or dialect. Your characters should code-switch when the teacher arrives on the scene and use more formal language.

Tip

Look back to Unit 4 to remind yourself how a drama script is laid out. Remember to use stage directions to show when characters enter or exit, and any sound effects.

Stretch yourself

When your drama is complete, write a paragraph to explain how and why the language changes as the scene progresses. Point out the differences between Standard English and non-standard English.

1: Texts all around us

1.8 What's the right tone?

In this unit, you will:

- learn how writers craft texts to persuade others to their viewpoint
- explore how writers use language and tone to influence their audience
- comment on the effect of language choices and tone in a speech.

What's the big idea?

In the previous units you have considered how writers choose the type of language they use, depending on their purpose and audience. You have also explored how people can best make their voices heard, and how knowing who is speaking or writing contributes to the impact of what they say or write. In this unit, you will learn how writers use language and tone to create powerful effects and influence their audience.

Activity 1

a In what ways do you think a writer is able to influence you as a reader? Can they make you feel or think in a certain way? Explain your answer.

b What difference does it make if someone talks or writes to you in an angry, excited or frustrated way?

c How can you tell what a writer or speaker is feeling just by reading or listening to them?

The extract opposite is from a speech presented to the United Nations Youth Assembly by Malala Yousafzai from Pakistan. The speech took place on her 16th birthday, and was less than a year after she was attacked by terrorists for speaking out about the right of girls to an education. The date of her speech has since been named Malala Day in her honour.

Did you know?

After she was attacked, Malala Yousafzai was treated in a British hospital and completed her education at Oxford University. She was awarded the Nobel Peace Prize in 2014 and continues to promote education for all.

Extract from Malala Yousafzai's speech to the UN, 2013

Today, it is an honour for me to be speaking again after a long time. Being here with such honourable people is a great moment in my life and it is an honour for me that today I am wearing a shawl of **Benazir Bhutto**. I don't know where to begin my speech. I don't know what people would be expecting me to say, but first of all thank you to God for whom we all are equal and thank you to every person who has prayed for my fast recovery and a new life. I cannot believe how much love people have shown me. I have received thousands of good wish cards and gifts from all over the world. Thank you to all of them. [...]

Dear brothers and sisters, do remember one thing. **Malala Day** is not my day. Today is the day of every woman, every boy, and every girl who have raised their voice for their rights. There are hundreds of human rights activists and social workers who are not only speaking for their rights, but who are struggling to achieve their goal of peace, education and equality. Thousands of people have been killed by the terrorists and millions have been injured. I'm just one of them. So here I stand. So here I stand, one girl, among many. I speak not for myself, but for those without voice can be heard. Those who have fought for their rights. Their right to live in peace. Their right to be treated with dignity. Their right to equality of opportunity. Their right to be educated.

Dear friends, on the 9th of October 2012, the **Taliban** shot me on the left side of my forehead. They shot my friends, too. They thought that the bullet would silence us, but they failed. And out of that silence came thousands of voices. The terrorists thought that they would change my aims and stop my ambitions. But nothing changed in my life except this: weakness, fear and hopelessness died. Strength, power and courage was born.

I am the same Malala. My ambitions are the same. My hopes are the same. And my dreams are the same. Dear sisters and brothers, I am not against anyone. Neither am I here to speak in terms of personal revenge against the Taliban or any other terrorist group. I am here to speak up for the right of education of every child. I want education for the sons and daughters of the Taliban and all the terrorists and **extremists**.

Benazir Bhutto – the prime minister of Pakistan from 1988–1990 and 1993–1996
Malala Day – on 12th July, the world celebrates Malala's birthday and supports the right of every child in every country to have access to free education
Taliban – an extremist religious and political movement in Pakistan and Afghanistan
extremists – people who hold an extreme opinion or view, particularly in politics

1: Texts all around us

⭐ Boosting your vocabulary

Writers choose their words carefully. The activity below focuses on some key vocabulary in the source text, which has been highlighted on page 55.

Activity 2

a   Malala opens her speech by saying 'Today it is *an honour* for me to be speaking again…' Choose a phrase from the list below with which you could replace the phrase 'an honour'.

   | a pleasure | a shame | a privilege | an embarrassment |

b   Malala repeats the words 'equal' and 'equality' in her speech. **'Equal'** is an adjective, meaning the same in value. **'Equality'** is a noun, meaning fairness for all.

   Take the adjectives listed below and turn them into nouns by adding the suffix 'ity'.

   | regular | fatal | real | hostile |

   Use each of the new nouns in a sentence to show you understand the meaning. For example:

   > When I looked at the soldier's face, I could see the hostility in his eyes.

c   Look at where Malala uses the word 'power' in her speech. It is part of a **tricolon** to **contrast** with 'weakness, fear and hopelessness'. Find another example of contrasting vocabulary in the text.

d   An activist is someone who is active in pursuing or promoting a cause. A terrorist is someone who uses violence and fear to pursue their purpose.

   Explain how Malala draws a contrast between the work of the activists and the activity of the terrorists.

🔑 Key terms

contrast to compare to show a difference

tricolon a pattern of three words or phrases grouped together to be memorable and have impact

1.8: What's the right tone?

Activity 3

In the speech, Malala is addressing the United Nations Youth Assembly. Millions of people have watched her speech online as well, so the audience is very wide and diverse.

a What do you think is the purpose of Malala's speech? Choose three or four phrases from the list below.

To entertain   To explain   To inspire   To advise   To inform

To persuade   To encourage   To describe   To thank

b Write a paragraph, using your chosen phrases, to explain the purpose and audience of the speech. You could start like this:

> There are several different reasons for Malala to make this speech to the United Nations Assembly. Firstly, she is thanking people…

Building your knowledge

Writers often express how they feel about their subject through the language they use. This is called the writer's tone. Adjectives describe the writer's tone, such as powerful, cheerful, aggressive or sarcastic.

We can identify Malala's tone by looking carefully at the words she chooses to use in her speech. In the first paragraph, Malala's tone sounds anxious, but also grateful. The tone is anxious because she repeats words such as 'I don't know', showing her uncertainty. The tone is also grateful in the phrase 'I have received thousands of good wish cards and gifts from all over the world'. The words 'thousands' and 'all over the world' emphasise how grateful she feels to have received so much goodwill.

Activity 4

a Which of the following adjectives describe the tone of the second, third and fourth paragraphs of Malala's speech?

determined and peaceful   defiant and courageous   humble and passionate

b Which words or phrases from each paragraph support your choice of tone?

57

1: Texts all around us

Activity 5

a   Read a paragraph of Malala's speech aloud with a change in the tone. For example, read the third paragraph nervously or the final paragraph aggressively.

b   How easy is it to change the tone of the text simply by using your voice?

c   Would it be easier to change the tone if you changed some of the words? If so, which ones?

d   How does the change in tone alter the effect on the audience?

> ✅ **Tip**
>
> The tone in writing is similar to the tone of your voice. It is not only *what* you say but *how* you say it.

The tone of a piece of writing can change the meaning of the texts you write. Let's take a topic such as: should people keep pets?

You could present your view on this topic using a critical or disapproving tone. Look at how the sample answer is annotated below.

> Keeping pets is *unbearably cruel.* People who keep pets are *unkind and inhuman.* They are *like prison guards* holding animals such as rabbits and hamsters captive in *tiny cages* and forgetting to feed them…

— Descriptions in the text show how the writer disapproves of keeping pets.

— This simile reinforces the disapproving tone.

Now look at another example from a writer with a different tone:

> Keeping pets is such a sweet thing to do. People who keep pets are so caring and compassionate. They care for their pets every day and in return have cuddles from their adorable fluffy companions.

Activity 6

a   List the words and phrases in the second example above that highlight the writer's feelings about people who keep pets.

b   Which words would you choose to describe the writer's tone in this text?

c   Write a short paragraph explaining how the writer's tone reveals their feelings about the subject of keeping pets.

1.8: What's the right tone?

Putting it all together

Activity 7

Read the text below and answer the following questions.

a Explain the purpose of this text.

b Who do you think is the audience for this text? Explain your answer with details from the text.

c Describe the writer's tone in this text. Select words and phrases from the text to support your description.

Extract from Air Ambulance charity website

West Midlands NHS support worker Ellie Milner was at the top of a remote hill in the Peak District when she had the most severe asthma attack of her life. Can you imagine how terrified she must have been?

5 Our critical care paramedics, doctors and pilots attend an average of ten emergency missions like this every day of the year. They help to provide urgent life-saving care due to accidents and medical emergencies at workplaces and sporting events, on the roads and in our homes. But on average, each mission costs £1,700.

10 That's an average of £8,500 every day to provide the life-saving services our community needs, services that are there for thousands of local people and their families.

Ellie was flown to the Northern General Hospital in Sheffield, where she was put on a life support machine for 48 hours. A few days later, Ellie "felt a lot better" and was able to attend a planned appointment with the
15 respiratory nurse specialist at the local hospital.

We hope that you, or someone you love, will never need our services, but if they do, please help us to be there.

Your donation today will help our life-saving critical care crews be there for more people like Ellie.

2 CRIME AND CONSEQUENCES

Crime fiction and writing about crime has been popular since the early 19th century. However, even before that, people have always been fascinated by crime and evil characters in stories. People not only want to know about the gruesome details of the crime, but also about the consequences. They want justice for the victims and for the perpetrator to be punished.

Readers have been introduced to many great detective characters, from Sherlock Holmes to Auguste Dupin and Hercule Poirot to Feluda. Writers use different language and structural techniques when writing about crime to provoke emotions in readers, whether it be sympathy or horror, even in true crime accounts, newspaper articles and poetry.

Use what you know

a Which fictional crime detectives have you heard of?

b Which crime mysteries have you read or watched?

c Choose two photos from the page and discuss what you see in them.

Words you need to know

tragedy, consequences, supernatural, intrigue, motive, suspects, reasoning, investigation, mystery, murder, detective, suspense, tension, convention, exposition, resolution

2: Crime and consequences

2 Learning overview

This learning overview will show you where the chapter will take you on your learning journey. Use it to help you plan your learning, monitor what you have learned and then evaluate your knowledge.

2.1 Why do we love crime fiction? 64–69

Prepare
- What do you already know about crime fiction?

What I will learn
- The genre of crime fiction.

How I will learn
- Identify genre conventions.
- Apply my understanding of genre to a writing plan.

2.2 What makes a character? 70–75

Prepare
- Do you know any fictional detectives?

What I will learn
- The techniques that writers use to present characters.

How I will learn
- Analyse characters from a text extract.

2.3 Who's telling the story? 76–81

Prepare
- What is a narrative voice?

What I will learn
- To identify and analyse narrative voices.

How I will learn
- Explore narrative voices in texts.
- Create a narrative voice in my writing.

2.4 Why all the tension? 82–87

Prepare
- When was the last time you felt suspense in a film or book?

What I will learn
- How authors create tension and suspense.
- The effect of structural and narrative devices on readers.

How I will learn
- Comment on how writers create tension and suspense.

2.5 What's the news? `88–93`

Prepare
- What do you know about newspaper writing and layouts?

What I will learn
- The structure and features of a news report.
- How to identify the writer's perspective.

How I will learn
- Write a crime news report.

2.6 What is figurative language? `94–99`

Prepare
- What makes you see images in your mind when you read a fiction book?

What I will learn
- To identify figurative language.
- How figurative language expresses a perspective.

How I will learn
- Comment on figurative language in a poem.

2.7 What's the difference? `100–105`

Prepare
- What are your two favourite books, films or TV shows?

What I will learn
- To compare texts.
- How to summarise the main points of texts.

How I will learn
- Compare how writers present perspective.

2.8 Can a text change your mind? `106–111`

Prepare
- What words do you use to persuade someone to agree with you?

What I will learn
- Techniques to make a perspective persuasive.

How I will learn
- Write and present a short paragraph in a debate.

63

2: Crime and consequences

2.1 Why do we love crime fiction?

In this unit, you will:

- learn about the genre of crime fiction
- identify genre conventions and explore how they impact on the reader
- write a plan for your own crime story.

What's the big idea?

Since ancient times, people have been fascinated by stories about characters who commit crimes, including the consequences of their actions, how justice is served and how order is restored. Our focus for this unit is the genre conventions of crime fiction and their impact on the reader.

The first crime **fiction** novels were written in the early 19th century. They focused on the discovery of a crime with a detective **character** investigating who had committed it, and why. The **genre** of crime fiction grew in popularity and particular **conventions** became associated with it.

It is important to be able to identify different genres because this helps us to understand what type of **text** we are reading, and what to expect from it. Every text fits into a genre and every genre has different conventions.

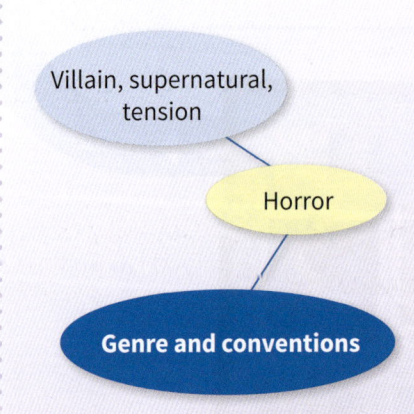

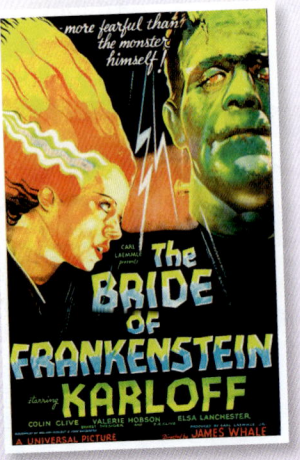

❓ Did you know?

Some elements of modern crime fiction can be traced back to Greek tragedies, where enthralled **audiences** watched the consequences of terrible crimes unfold.

🔑 Key terms

audience the people or person for whom a text is written or performed

character a person in a drama or story

convention a typical feature you find in a particular genre

fiction a narrative that is imaginary or invented

genre a type of story, e.g. *horror, romance, adventure, science fiction*

text any form of written material

⚙ Activity 1

Draw a mind map showing the different genres you can think of and some of the conventions you might expect to find in each.

- Villain, supernatural, tension
- Horror
- **Genre and conventions**

64

2.1: Why do we love crime fiction?

The article below explores why people are fascinated by crime stories. As you read it, think about what the author is saying about how crime fiction influences the way a reader thinks and feels.

Four Reasons We Love Binging Crime Shows

We might be wired to love true crime.

Watching crime television and murder mysteries is kind of like witnessing a car crash: it's hard to look at, but it's also hard to look away. There is a level of disgust that we experience while watching or listening to these stories of violence and terror, and yet we keep coming back for more [...] but why are these dark, twisted stories so popular with audiences across the globe?

1. We love a good adrenaline rush.

Crime shows let us get a hearty **adrenaline** rush in the comfort of our own home. Adrenaline is something that we seek out on a daily basis, whether it be through playing a sport, climbing a mountain, or seeking out a crime thriller. Like a rollercoaster, true-crime series let us feel a **simulated** fear that we know poses no real threat.

2. Our mind and imagination are engaged.

Crime entertainment is like working a puzzle that also gives you a rush of excitement every time you put the last piece in. These series are often presented in a play-by-play mystery format, where the viewer is solving the case alongside the detectives. These shows and podcasts stimulate us intellectually and leave us with a sense of satisfaction afterward, as if we played a role in bringing justice.

3. We are wired to enjoy true crime.

Or rather, true crime is wired for us to enjoy. Evolution has sharpened humans' survival instincts to the point where it feels natural and sometimes enjoyable to, well, survive. [...] Crime-based entertainment is made to activate our survival instincts. [...] As a result, we enjoy our 'close calls' with danger as we experience the stories unfolding before us.

4. We are fascinated by our own 'dark side'.

As non-violent members of society, we are **appalled** by the thought of committing the terrible acts that [...] criminals are known for. To imagine carrying out such acts ourselves is nearly impossible; yet why do we find it so intriguing?

Another human – the very same as you and me – committed horrific crimes, and the fact that all humans are **hypothetically** capable of this is astonishing.

In crime shows, we watch someone else act upon their taboo thoughts, indulging in what most of us dare not let our minds wander to. Viewers, in turn, find ourselves fascinated with our own **capacity** to possess these taboo sides, horrified yet intrigued by what we are capable of. Simply put, we love to safely observe our own dark capabilities without any consequences.

---

adrenaline – a hormone released by excitement or fear that causes the heart to beat faster
simulated – artificial or made-up
appalled – feeling a strong sense of disgust
intriguing – fascinating
hypothetically – supposedly, in theory
capacity – ability

2: Crime and consequences

★ Boosting your vocabulary

Writers choose their words carefully. The activity below focuses on some key vocabulary in the source text, which has been highlighted on page 65.

Activity 2

a   Our feelings can be 'stimulated' by the things we read. What feelings might be stimulated by reading the texts below?
   - a horror story
   - a romance novel
   - a newspaper report about a murder

b   i   Are the words 'stimulate' and 'intrigue' **synonyms**? Explain your answer.
   ii   What synonyms can you think of for the words 'stimulate' and 'intrigue'?

c   If something is 'taboo' it is avoided, forbidden or banned, although not necessarily against the law. For example, swearing or using a mobile phone during a lesson might be taboo.
   i   Note down some more examples of things that are taboo.
   ii   Why do you think we like to read about taboo acts?

🔑 Key term

synonym a word or phrase that means the same, or almost the same, as another word or phrase

Activity 3

a   Summarise in your own words the four reasons the writer gives for why people enjoy the crime genre.

b   What different feelings does the author say we experience when we watch or read crime fiction? Are these feelings positive or negative? Explain why.

⬆ Stretch yourself

'Watching or reading about crime could encourage people to commit criminal acts.' Do you agree or disagree with this statement? What do you think the author of the article would say? Find evidence in the text to support your point of view.

2.1: Why do we love crime fiction?

Building your knowledge

Crime fiction can include some or all of the conventions below.

- A cunning detective. If they are a private detective, they are usually cleverer than the police. Sometimes the detective is conventionally attractive and has a love interest in the story.
- An assistant to the detective who may narrate (tell) the story but is not as cunning as the detective.
- A crime that seems impossible to solve.
- A villain who has committed a crime and needs to be caught before they reoffend.
- A remote or secluded **setting**, such as a house in the countryside.
- Many different characters staying in a place where a crime is committed. All the characters have their own secrets and are possible suspects.
- Many 'red herrings' (false clues), included to confuse the reader.
- A **climax** in which the cunning detective reveals the truth and solves the crime.

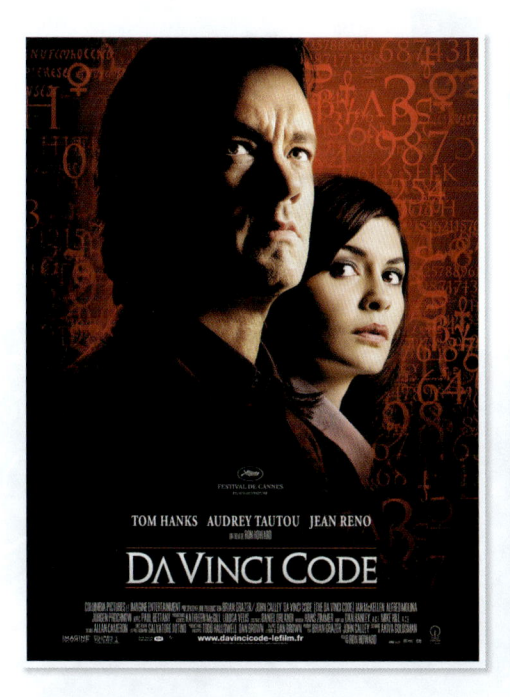

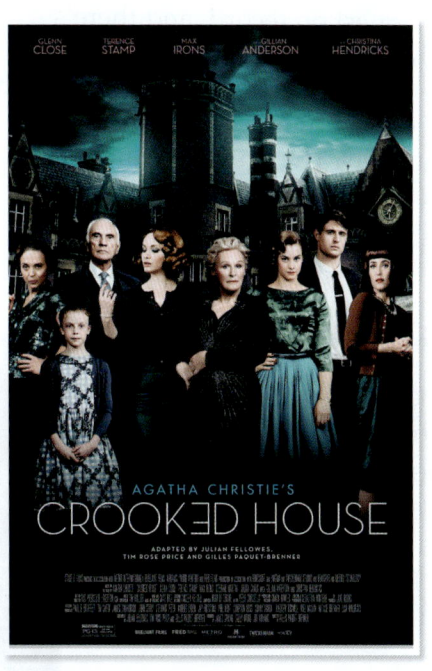

Key terms

climax when the action is at its most exciting or interesting

setting where the action takes place

Did you know?

A 'locked room mystery' is a type of crime fiction in which a crime has taken place that seems to have been impossible to commit, for example a murder in a locked room.

Activity 4

Look carefully at the posters for film adaptations of famous crime novels above. What conventions from the list above can you identify in these posters?

67

2: Crime and consequences

Activity 5

a Read the blurbs from the crime fiction books below and identify the conventions in each story.

b Pick one blurb. What emotions does this blurb stimulate in the reader?

Complete the sentence starters below as part of your answer.

> The author uses the conventions of…
>
> These are effective because they make the reader…
>
> The author has created intrigue because I have questions I'd like to find out the answers to, such as…

High Rise Mystery
by Sharna Jackson

Summer in London is hot, the hottest on record, and there's been a murder in The Tri: the high-rise home to resident know-it-alls Nik and Norva. Who better to solve the case? Armed with curiosity, home-turf knowledge and unlimited time – until the end of the summer holidays anyway. The first whodunnit in a new mystery series by Sharna Jackson.

Murder at the Dolphin Hotel **by Helena Dixon**

June 1933. Kitty Underhay is a modern, independent woman […]. She prides herself on the reputation of her family's ancient hotel on the blustery English coast. But then a body is found, rooms are ransacked and rumours begin to circulate that someone is on the hunt for a valuable stolen ruby – a ruby that Kitty's mother may have possessed when she herself went missing during the First World War.

When the local police inspector shows no signs of solving the shocking crimes plaguing the hotel, Kitty steps briskly into the breach. Together with ox army captain Matthew Bryant, her new hotel security officer, she is determined to decipher this mystery and preserve not only the name of her hotel, but also the lives of her guests.

2.1: Why do we love crime fiction?

**Arsenic For Tea: A Murder Most Unladylike Mystery
by Robin Stevens**

Schoolgirl detectives Daisy Wells and Hazel Wong are at Daisy's home, Fallingford, for the holidays. Daisy's glamorous mother is throwing a tea party for Daisy's birthday, and the whole family is invited. Then one of their party falls seriously, mysteriously ill – and everything points to poison.

With wild storms preventing anyone from leaving, or the police from arriving, Fallingford suddenly feels like a very dangerous place to be. Not a single person present is what they seem – and everyone has a secret or two. And when someone very close to Daisy looks suspicious, the Detective Society must do everything they can to reveal the truth… no matter the consequences.

Putting it all together

Activity 6

Use the knowledge you have learned from exploring the conventions of crime fiction to write a plan for your own crime story. You should include at least five different conventions.

a   Complete a plan like the one started below.

> Setting: a country house in Yorkshire for a birthday celebration of an elderly aunt
>
> Characters: elderly aunt, young and confident niece, untrustworthy brother, Detective Pierce
>
> Crime/mystery:
>
> Solution:

b   Share your plan with a partner. Ask your partner to identify the conventions you have included. What feelings does your plan stimulate in your partner? Why?

> **✓ Tip**
>
> If you need a reminder, refer back to the list of conventions in the Building your knowledge section on page 67.

2: Crime and consequences

2.2 What makes a character?

In this unit, you will:
- learn about the techniques writers use to present characters
- explore explicit and implicit information
- analyse how a character is presented.

What's the big idea?
Believable, interesting characters play a big part in drawing readers into all stories. In crime fiction, readers have to believe in the power of the detective and the evilness of the villain. Our focus in this unit is on how writers create believable characters – the techniques they use, how we can identify these techniques and their effects on the reader.

Activity 1

a What makes a great detective? List your ideas. (Think about any detectives you know in books or films. They might be adults or young people.)

b Based on your knowledge of crime fiction conventions, what do you predict we will learn about the detective in this unit?

Did you know?
One of the first popular crime stories for young people was *Emil and the Detectives*, written by Erich Kästner in 1929. Stories about groups of children working together to solve mysteries and catch criminals grew in popularity in the 20th century and include novels by Enid Blyton.

In 1841, Edgar Allan Poe published 'The Murders in the Rue Morgue'. It was one of the first crime stories published. The conventions Poe used and his key detective character Auguste Dupin, inspired many other authors, such as Arthur Conan Doyle, the creator of Sherlock Holmes. Poe played a key role in creating the genre of crime fiction as we know it today.

As you read the text opposite, think about the different conventions of crime fiction you can identify and what you learn about the detective.

Edgar Allan Poe

Extract from 'The Murders in the Rue Morgue' by Edgar Allan Poe

Dupin was the last member of a well-known family, a family which had once been rich and famous; he himself, however, was far from rich. He cared little about money. He had enough to buy the most necessary things of life – and a few books; he did not trouble himself about the rest. Just books. With books he was happy.

We first met when we were both trying to find the same book. As it was a book which few had ever heard of, this chance brought us together in an old bookstore.

[...]

We **passed the days** reading, writing and talking. But Dupin was a lover of the night, and at night, often with only the light of the stars to show us the way, we walked the streets of Paris, sometimes talking, sometimes quiet, always thinking.

I soon noticed a special reasoning power he had, an unusual reasoning power. Using it gave him great pleasure. He told me once, with a soft and quiet laugh, that most men have windows over their hearts; through these he could see into their souls. Then, he surprised me by telling what he knew about my own soul; and I found that he knew things about me that I had thought only I could possibly know. His manner at these moments was cold and distant. His eyes looked empty and far away, and his voice became high and nervous. At such times it seemed to me that I saw not just Dupin, but two Dupins – one who coldly put things together, and another who just as coldly took them apart.

One night we were walking down one of Paris's long and dirty streets. Both of us were busy with our thoughts. Neither had spoken for perhaps fifteen minutes. It seemed as if we had each forgotten that the other was there, at his side. I soon learned that Dupin had not forgotten me, however. Suddenly he said: "You're right. He is a very little fellow, that's true, and he would be more successful if he acted in lighter, less serious plays."

"Yes, there can be no doubt of that!" I said. At first I saw nothing strange in this. Dupin had agreed with me, with my own thoughts. This, of course, seemed to me quite natural. For a few seconds I continued walking, and thinking; but suddenly I realised that Dupin had agreed with something which was only a thought. I had not spoken a single word. I stopped walking and turned to my friend. "Dupin," I said. "Dupin, this is beyond my understanding. How could you know that I was thinking of ...?"

---

passed the days – spent time

2: Crime and consequences

⭐ Boosting your vocabulary

Writers choose their words carefully. The activity below focuses on some key vocabulary in the source text, which has been highlighted on page 71.

> **Key terms**
>
> **antonym** a word that has the opposite meaning of a particular word
>
> **connotation** an idea or feeling linked to a word, as well as its main meaning
>
> **narrator** a person who tells a story, especially in a book, play or film

Activity 2

a To act 'coldly' or to be described as a 'cold' person means 'seems to have no feelings'. Think of two synonyms and two **antonyms** for the word 'cold' based on how it is used in the extract.

b If a person is 'distant', they seem not to connect with another person when they talk to them and don't show much emotion. What is the effect of someone being cold and distant? Explain your answer carefully, giving some examples.

c What **connotations** do the words 'cold' and 'distant' convey, when used to describe a character? What might they suggest about physical appearance and other characteristics?

d A person who has good 'reasoning' skills has learned to work out the solution to problems and understand difficult concepts. Why is this an important skill for a detective?

e The **narrator** describes Dupin as having a 'special reasoning power'. What do you think he means by the word 'power' in this context?

Activity 3

a What conventions of crime writing did you find in this text? (Use the list on page 67 to help you.) Why do you think Poe uses them?

b Can you identify and explain three reasons why Dupin is likely to be a good detective?

72

2.2: What makes a character?

Building your knowledge

When writers create characters, they use a variety of techniques to help the reader to imagine them as fully as possible. They want the reader to imagine how the character looks, what they are like as a person, how they sound and how they treat other people. Writers want the reader to feel they *know* the character, as if they are real. The way that a writer presents a character for a reader is called **characterisation**.

A writer can choose to give **explicit** information about a character. This means they tell the reader directly and clearly what they want them to know, for example, 'he had long, wavy hair'.

A writer might also give the reader **implicit** information about a character. This means that the writer is implying or hinting at other, more subtle details about a character. The reader has to **infer** what this additional information means and build up their own interpretation. For example, 'she looked away uneasily' could imply the character feels uncomfortable or is hiding something.

It's important to be able to identify the techniques a writer uses to create a character so we can appreciate the writer's craft, analyse how these techniques impact on the reader, and learn how to use these techniques in our own writing.

Key terms

characterisation the methods an author uses to create a character, e.g. describing how they look, the use of dialogue or showing how they treat others

explicit stating something openly and exactly

implicit not stated directly, but suggested or hinted at

infer to work something out from what is seen, said or done, even though it is not stated directly

Activity 4

Read the sentences below. What explicit information is given in this description of a young detective and what can you infer?

> She hesitated at the doorway, pulling her shabby coat more tightly around her small frame. She took a deep breath, then, with her head held high, she stepped forward into the room full of uniformed officers and cleared her throat.

2: Crime and consequences

Activity 5

Look back at the extract from 'The Murders in the Rue Morgue'. Think carefully about the techniques that the writer has used to convey the character of Dupin.

a Complete a table like the one below. The first row has been completed for you.

Characterisation technique	Evidence in the text	What impression does it create for the reader (implicit or explicit)?
Giving background information	'last member of a well-known family… which had once been rich and famous'; 'he himself … was far from rich.'	Explicit information about Dupin's finances, but it makes the reader curious about how the family money had been lost.
Description of his values and interests		
Physical description (of his eyes)		
Description of his voice		
Dialogue (relationship with the narrator)		
The use of imagery, such as **metaphor**		

b Choose one or two characterisation techniques and explain how the writer uses them in the extract and the effect they create for the reader.

✓ Tip

You might find some of the following words and sentence starters useful.

This suggests…   This implies…
This could show…   The reader could feel…
This might make the reader question…
The reader can imagine…   intriguing
stimulates   intelligent   friendship
kind   unfeeling

🔑 Key terms

dialogue words spoken by characters
metaphor a comparison that says one thing *is* something else, e.g. *Amy was a rock*

2.2: What makes a character?

Putting it all together

Activity 6

Using some of the information you gathered in your table during Activity 5, answer the following question:

> How does Poe present the character of Dupin as likeable but a bit unusual?

Follow the steps below.

Step 1: Discuss the following questions.
- Is Dupin likeable or do you dislike his character? What evidence supports your idea?
- Do you think Dupin is a bit unusual? What evidence supports your idea?

Step 2: Plan your answer.
You may find it helpful to complete a table like the one below.

Dupin	Evidence in the text	What impression does it create for the reader (implicit or explicit)?
Likeable/dislikable		
Unusual		

Step 3: Read an extract from a student's answer below, along with the teacher's comment.

> I think Dupin is a bit unusual because Poe says he has 'special reasoning power', 'an unusual reasoning power'. Poe says it is 'special' and 'unusual', which suggests not everyone is like Dupin. He also says Dupin was 'a lover of the night'. This is unusual because many people don't like darkness. Being in the dark might suggest Dupin has something to hide or that he doesn't like being around other people or being seen by them, which is unusual; so I agree that he is a bit unusual.

This is a good explanation because you have used three quotations from the text. I like the way you have embedded the quotations in your own sentences. You have also explained clearly what each piece of evidence suggests or implies about Dupin and focused on the question. Well done!

Step 4: From looking at this answer, write down three things that you feel will help you to make your own answer successful.

Step 5: Write your own answer to the question in full. Use the information in the table you completed earlier.

2: Crime and consequences

2.3 Who's telling the story?

In this unit, you will:
- learn to identify and analyse narrative voices
- explore the effect of different narrative voices on the reader
- create your own narrative voice.

What's the big idea?

A narrative voice is the voice that writers create to tell their story. There are different types of narrative voice that have various effects on the reader. In this unit we're going to look in more detail at how authors create a narrative voice and think about how we can use these techniques in our own writing.

Some authors write in the voice of their main character and use first-person pronouns such as I, me, we and us. We call this a **first-person narrative**.

Other writers tell the story using third-person pronouns such as they, he and she. We call this a **third-person narrative**; it can tell the story from the perspective of just one character, or the writer can use several different perspectives.

Activity 1

a What are some of the most memorable narrative voices you have read or seen?

b Look at the **quotations** below and the descriptions of the voice speaking. Match each quotation to the description that you think is most appropriate.

"OMG can you believe he said that? It's out of order and I'm gonna tell him!"

formal, serious, judgemental, elderly and grave

"Perhaps one would be wise to consider how one's actions affect those around one. It is not for the few to decide for the many."

informal, dramatic, opinionated and angry

Key terms

first-person narrative a story told by someone as if they were involved in the events themselves, using first-person pronouns, e.g. *I* and *we*

inciting incident the event that sets up the action for the rest of the story

narrative voice the perspective (viewpoint) from which a story is told, and the style in which it is told

quotation a word or phrase from a text

third-person narrative a story told by someone who was not involved in the events themselves, using third-person pronouns, e.g. *he, she, they*

2.3: Who's telling the story?

Smart is a murder mystery novel where the main character Kieran is the narrator. In this extract, Kieran finds a dead body; this **inciting incident** sparks a murder investigation. As you read, think about what sort of information the author implies about Kieran's character through his **narrative voice**.

Extract from *Smart* by Kim Slater

It just looked like a pile of rags, floating on the water.

Jean sat on the bench with the brass plaque on. It said: *In Memory of Norman Reeves, who spent many happy hours here.*

The plaque means Norman Reeves is dead, but it doesn't actually say that.

5 Jean held her head in her hands and her body was all jerky, like when you are laughing or crying. I guessed she was crying and I was right.

"He was my friend," she sobbed.

I looked around but Jean was alone. [...]

"Who?" I asked.

10 Jean pointed to the rags.

I went to the edge of the embankment to look. There was a stripy bag half in the water. I saw a face with a bushy beard in the middle of the rags, under the ripples. One eye was open, one was closed. I freaked out. The sea sound started in my head and I ran right past the bridge and back again but there was nobody to help. I'm not supposed to run like mad because it can start my asthma off.

15 "When the sea noise comes in your head," Miss Crane says, "it is important to stay calm and breathe."

I stopped running. I tried to stay calm and breathe. I used my inhaler.

Jean was still crying when I got back.

"He was my friend," she said again. I picked up a long stick and took it over to the riverbank. I poked at the face but not near the eyes.

20 "What are you doing?" Jean shouted from the bench.

"I'm doing a test to see if it's a balloon," I yelled back. It felt puffy and hard at the same time, so I knew it was Jean's friend's head.

"Is it a balloon?" shouted Jean.

A woman with a dog was coming.

25 When she got near I said, "Jean's friend is in the river."

She gave me a funny look, like she might ignore me and carry on walking. Then she came a bit nearer and looked at the river. She started screaming.

I went for a walk up the embankment to stay calm and breathe. Some Canada geese flew down and skidded into the water. They didn't care about the rags and the puffy face. They just got on with it.

30 When I got back, a policeman and a policewoman were talking to the lady with the dog. Jean was still sitting on the bench but nobody was talking to her.

"That's him," the woman said, and pointed at me.

"What's your name, son?" the policeman asked.

"I'm not your son," I said.

2: Crime and consequences

⭐ Boosting your vocabulary

Writers choose their words carefully. The activity below focuses on some key vocabulary in the source text, which has been highlighted on page 77.

> **Key term**
>
> **verb** a word or group of words that express an action, event or state, e.g. the boy *eats*, tigers *prowl*, the building *exists*

Activity 2

a The characters are shocked and upset by what they have seen in the water. The author uses these **verbs** to describe their reactions:

   sobbed   screaming   running

   What are the connotations of these verbs?

   For example:

   > The word 'sobbed' suggests she is very upset and no one can make her feel better.

b Imagine you have seen something really shocking. Write a sentence or two using three verbs to describe your reaction. Think carefully about the connotations of the words you choose.

c In the text, Kieran says he 'freaked out'. This is informal vocabulary. What more formal synonyms (words or phrases) could you use to describe how Kieran feels?

d Re-read lines 28–29. Pick out another informal phrase that most people understand but would not use in a formal situation.

💡 Building your knowledge

When creating a narrative voice, writers have to think carefully about what they want that voice to convey to the reader. Different types of narrative voice establish a different relationship with the reader and affect how the reader thinks about the characters and events that are described.

2.3: Who's telling the story?

Activity 3

a Rewrite these sentences from the extract as a third-person narrative.

> I freaked out. The sea sound started in my head and I ran right past the bridge and back again but there was nobody to help. I'm not supposed to run like mad because it can start my asthma off.

Start with:

> He freaked out. The sea sound started in his head…

b How does this new version change the reader's feelings towards Kieran? Think about how close you feel to him, how sympathetic you feel, and the level of drama.

As well as choosing what type of narrator to use, a writer has to decide on the **tone** and **register** of the narrative voice. This is particularly true in a first-person narrative but applies to third-person narratives too. The tone can show the reader what the character's feelings and attitudes are – for example, they might be bored, frightened or entertained by what happens. The register of the narrative voice can vary between formal, neutral and informal language, but a writer should try to ensure the register of the voice is consistent throughout, to help build up a clear picture of how the character's mind works.

Key terms

register the manner of speaking or writing, which can range between formal and informal

tone the writer's feeling or attitude expressed towards their subject; in fiction it can also reflect a character's feelings and personality

Activity 4

a How would you describe the tone of the narrative voice in the extract on page 77? Use at least one quotation from the extract to explain your answer. You might want to choose a tone from the list below.

excited   disturbed   frightened   cautious   confused

b What sort of register does the writer use for Kieran's narrative voice? Does he speak in a formal, complex way, or does he use more informal, simpler language? Use two quotations from the extract to explain your answer.

Stretch yourself

What else do you notice about Kieran's narrative voice? Think about whether it sounds knowledgeable, humorous, childlike, imaginative or simplistic.

79

2: Crime and consequences

A first-person narrative voice is particularly good for revealing information about the character of the narrator, what sort of person they are and how they handle emotions. This information about the character is often implied and it's up to us, the readers, to infer what it means.

Activity 5

a   What does the narrative voice reveal about Kieran's character? Complete a table like the one below.

Evidence from the text	What it reveals about Kieran's character
'I tried to stay calm and breathe. I used my inhaler.'	
' "What's your name, son?" the policeman asked. "I'm not your son," I said.'	
' "I'm doing a test to see if it's a balloon," I yelled back.'	

b   Write a paragraph explaining what you think of Kieran's character.
   i   Identify parts of the text that make you feel this way.
   ii How do you think the writer wants you to feel towards Kieran? Why?

c   Continue the extract by writing a few sentences in the same narrative voice as Kieran. Remember to keep the same style in terms of tone and register. Think carefully about what he says and *how* he says it.

You could use one of the sentence starters below or think of your own.

"Don't be cheeky," said …

"My dad is…"

The policeman looked cross but I didn't…

> **Tip**
>
> Look back at page 73 to remind yourself about implicit information and how to infer.

80

2.3: Who's telling the story?

Putting it all together

Activity 6

Imagine you are going to write the crime story you planned in unit 1. Your crime story will need a detective. What sort of person are they?

a   Complete a 'role on the wall' for your detective character. Draw the outline of a person and on the inside write the thoughts, feelings, likes and dislikes of your character. On the outside, write down key facts about your character, for example their age, name, past experiences, family.

b   Now that you have created your own detective character, think about the narrative voice you will use. Your detective could be telling their own story as a first-person narrator.

- Think about what sort of detective they are. How old are they? Are they very ordered and precise or are they a bit chaotic? How might this affect their narrative voice?
- What sort of register will your narrative voice have? What tone do you want to create? How will this impact on your vocabulary and sentence structure?
- How do you want your reader to feel about your detective character?

c   Write a paragraph of your crime story in which your detective looks around the crime scene. Focus on creating a narrative voice that reveals what sort of person your detective is.

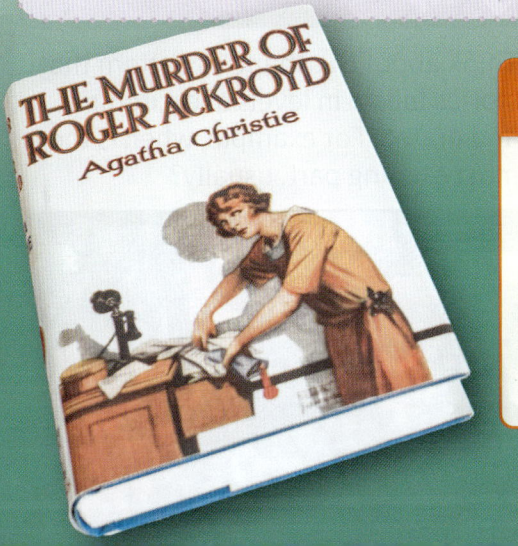

Name: Alisha Ahmed
Lives alone in Manchester
Eats pizza three nights a week
Has a pet cat that goes everywhere with her
35 years old
Sometimes lonely
Hates people whose brains don't work as quickly as hers
Always wears a sharp black jacket and thick glasses
Reads seven books a week
Has long black hair, always worn in a ponytail, sometimes covered by a headscarf
Loves solving mysteries
Has one friend, Hassan Amar, who has known her forever
Doesn't like to talk about her family

? Did you know?

Sometimes writers create **unreliable narrators**. This means the narrative voice is one that the reader cannot trust. A famous example is in Agatha Christie's book *The Murder of Roger Ackroyd* in which the narrator deliberately misleads the reader.

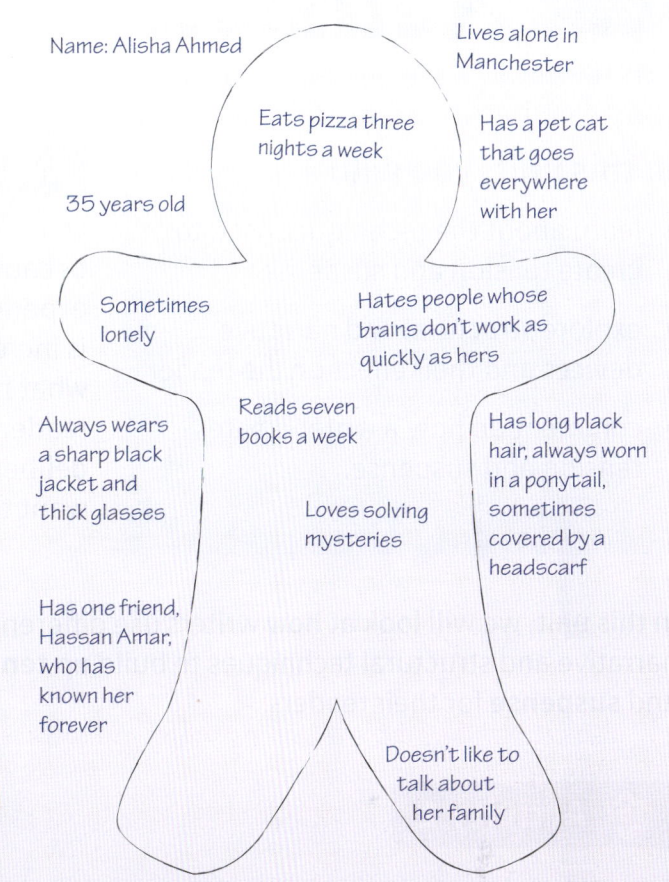

🔑 Key term

unreliable narrator a narrator who may or may not prove to be trustworthy, either intentionally or otherwise

81

2: Crime and consequences

2.4 Why all the tension?

In this unit, you will:
- learn about the techniques used to create tension and suspense
- explore structural and narrative devices and their effect on the reader
- comment on how a writer creates tension and suspense.

What's the big idea?
One reason that many readers love crime fiction is because it gives them the excitement of danger without experiencing real fear for themselves. The sense of danger is increased by not knowing exactly what is going on, or what has happened or what may still happen. Keeping the reader guessing is a key feature of crime fiction. Writers deliberately create tension and suspense, so that readers want to read on.

In this unit, we will look at how writers use different narrative and structural techniques to build up **tension** and **suspense** for their readers.

Activity 1

a What do you already know about the structure of most stories?

b From what you know about the crime fiction genre, what sort of techniques do you predict a writer might use to create tension and suspense? For example, what effect might a **cliffhanger**, or a lot of questions from a character, have on a reader?

Key terms

cliffhanger an exciting event at the end of a chapter, leaving the reader anxious and eager to know what happens next

suspense a feeling of anxious uncertainty while waiting for something to happen or become known

tension a feeling of being on edge with nerves stretched tight

The extract opposite is taken from *Murder in Midwinter* by Fleur Hitchcock. Maya is on a bus and sees something troubling…

As you read, think about:
- how the writer sets the scene
- how the writer lays out the text
- what happens at the end and how the reader feels.

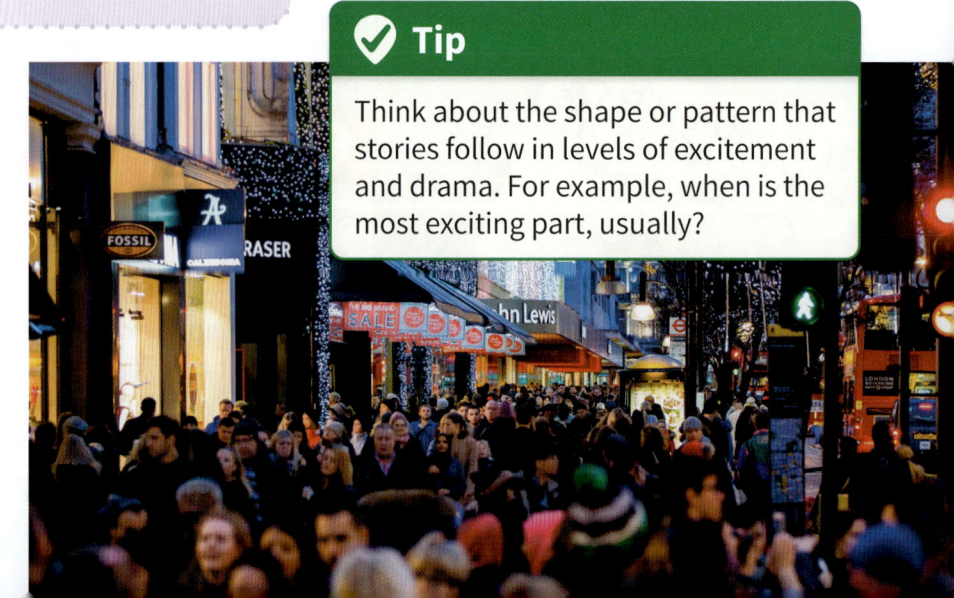

Tip
Think about the shape or pattern that stories follow in levels of excitement and drama. For example, when is the most exciting part, usually?

82

2.4: Why all the tension?

Extract from *Murder in Midwinter* by Fleur Hitchcock

The bus makes a dash over a set of lights and I find myself staring at a new set of shoppers. We head towards one of the huge Christmas window displays and I get my phone on to the camera setting so that I can take a picture for Zahra. It's difficult to get a decent shot, there are so many people in the way, but I hold it up ready to click. We judder to a halt and I start taking photos even though the windows are slightly further ahead.

Click

Flash

Click

Flash

Click

Click

What was that?

Click

Looking through the viewfinder, I see a man. He's in a gap in the crowd. He's tall, with curly hair. Ginger hair, I think. Everyone else seems to be rushing past him but I notice him because he's standing still. There's a woman there, she's still too. They're arguing. He disappears as the crowd swirls around him. A couple with shopping bags swing across the view, some kids, a large family, but my eye goes back to the man the moment he reappears.

Click

Click

He's holding something.

Click

Is that a gun? He's drawn a gun on her?

I keep taking the photos, and the flash goes off half the time and then the man looks at me and so does she. I take another photo and he runs and the bus pulls away, stop-starting through the crowds all the way down to **Piccadilly Circus**.

I stare back up the pavement but I can't even see the lights of the department store now. The woman next to me gets off, and a bloke reading a book gets on. It's all really normal, but what have I just seen?

Was that a gun or not?

I flick through the photos.

There are quite a few where the flash just reflects on the window, one really good one of the window display, and then three blurry pics of the man and the woman. Two from the side, one straight on, looking right at me. I zoom in on his hand.

Definitely a gun. Or definitely the barrel of a gun.

A man holding a gun? In **Regent Street**, ten days before Christmas.

The time on the photo is 17.14. It's only 17.26.

I swallow, feel sick, excited then terrified. I doubt myself.

Piccadilly Circus, Regent Street – busy places in central London

2: Crime and consequences

⭐ Boosting your vocabulary

Writers choose their words carefully. The activity below focuses on some key vocabulary in the source text, which has been highlighted on page 83.

Activity 2

a   Find these words in the text:

   swirls   dash   rushing   swing

   What type of words are these? What impression do they create for the reader?

b   Think of some other words that could be used to describe a busy place, such as a crowd at a festival. Write a few sentences to set another scene, in which a dramatic event might be about to happen. Include the words you have chosen.

c   What word does the writer use twice to **contrast** all this movement? Why is this choice effective?

d   Find the word 'reflects' in the text. This verb can have two meanings. What are they?

e   The words below all start with the **prefix** 're-', which means 'again' or 'back again'. Think of two more words that you could add to this list. Write a definition for each word.

   reflect   revisit   revise   relocate   reclaim

f   The writer uses vocabulary to show us how Maya feels about what she has seen: 'excited', 'terrified', 'doubt'.
   i   Come up with two synonyms for each word. Remember your synonyms should imply strong emotions and confusion.
   ii Find one antonym for each word.
   iii Write a sentence containing at least two of these antonyms, describing how you might feel in another situation.

🔑 Key terms

contrast to compare to show a difference

prefix a word or group of letters placed in front of another word to add to or change its meaning

✅ Tip

For the second meaning, consider a way of thinking.

2.4: Why all the tension?

Building your knowledge

Text structure refers to how writers order and organise the information they give to the reader. In crime fiction, the writer wants to keep the reader guessing, so they use the structure of their text to create as much tension and suspense as possible.

Crime fiction usually follows the same structure, going through five main stages spread over three 'acts'. These stages are: the introduction, rising action, the climax, falling action, and the ending (resolution).

> **? Did you know?**
>
> The three-act structure is used for most Hollywood films and TV dramas, so it doesn't just apply to crime fiction!

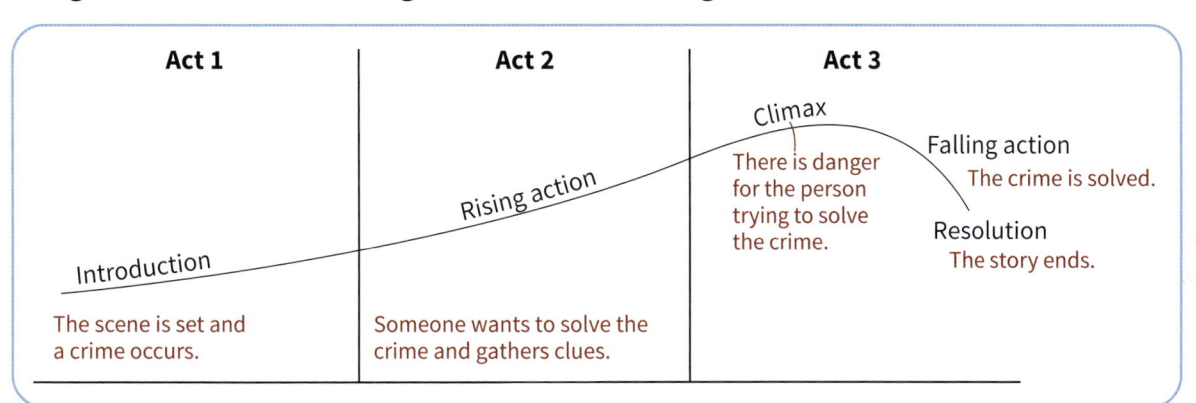

Act 1 — Introduction: The scene is set and a crime occurs.

Act 2 — Rising action: Someone wants to solve the crime and gathers clues.

Act 3 — Climax: There is danger for the person trying to solve the crime. Falling action: The crime is solved. Resolution: The story ends.

Activity 3

a Think of a crime story that follows this structure. It might be a book you have read, or a film or a TV show. Explain what happens at each stage.

b Think about the extract from *Murder in Midwinter*. Where do you think this extract fits into the whole structure of the story? Give reasons for your answer.

The start of a story should make the reader curious, perhaps ask a lot of questions and feel there is a challenge to work out or a puzzle to solve. Crime writers tend to use a detective character to ask a lot of questions – questions that the reader would also like answers to. For example:

> Lemn frowned at the scene. How could anyone have got into the vault? The locks were still secure. Why were the jewellery boxes gone but the diamonds left on the floor?

Activity 4

Imagine a crime scene and a detective arriving. Write a few sentences about what they observe and what questions spring to mind.

85

2: Crime and consequences

As the crime story unfolds, writers often include cliffhangers. Immediately after a dramatic event the writer switches to focus on something else, or starts a new chapter. This type of delay in revealing what happens next creates tension and makes the reader keen to read on to find out. For example:

> She gripped the window ledge with her fingertips and wedged her toes into a small gulley between the stone panels. She would hang on. Help was coming.
>
> Then she felt the ancient stone crumble.

Writers can control the tension and suspense in a text by varying the **pace** of the narrative. Using a mix of short and longer sentences can help to speed up or slow down the narrative, reflecting the mood or the action. For example:

> Tick. Tick. Tick. The sun glared through the window. The air was still. Time stopped. I held my breath. Until... The bell rang! Like a shot, I ran out of the room, down the stairs, round the corner, past the vending machine, dodging crowds and teachers until I finally, FINALLY, made it to the freedom of the playing field, where I knew I could share my exciting discovery with the others.

🔑 **Key term**

pace the speed at which someone moves or something happens

Activity 5

Look back at the extract from *Murder in Midwinter*. What techniques has the writer used to build up tension and suspense? Complete a table like the one below. The first row has been completed for you.

Narrative techniques	Evidence in the text	How does this build up tension and suspense for the reader?
Setting the scene (using contrasts in description)	Words such as 'swirls', 'dash', 'rushing' build up a picture of movement of crowds. The word 'still' provides contrast.	The sudden focus on two people, who are standing still in the crowd, draws the focus to them and makes the reader curious and alert to something strange going on.
A character's questions		
Varying the pace		

86

2.4: Why all the tension?

🧩 Putting it all together

When writing about a text, it is important that you can identify the techniques that the writer has used in order to create certain effects for the reader. In crime fiction, many of these techniques are specifically designed to 'hook' the attention of the reader, then create tension and suspense throughout the story, so that readers are keen to read on.

Activity 6

Read the question below.

> How and why does the author create tension and suspense for the reader in this extract?

a Look at this example response from a student. Read the annotations to understand how they have structured their response.

> The author 'hooks' the reader in by using lots of short sentences and single-word paragraphs, for example 'Click', 'Flash'. This makes the pace seem slow because there is a lot of repetition. But then the single repeated words are interrupted with 'What was that?' and this makes the reader want to know what the narrator has seen and keep reading to find out more. The author might be withholding information on purpose to create tension for the reader.

- Identifies the narrative technique.
- Explores what the narrative technique does.
- Analyses how this technique impacts on the reader.

b Now it's your turn to answer the same question, but in more detail. In your answer you should consider:

- why the action occurs in this order
- what techniques the writer uses – refer to examples in the text
- what these techniques make the reader feel and understand
- how these techniques support the author's intentions.

✅ Tip

Remember to use the information you gathered in Activity 5 to help you answer this question.

87

2: Crime and consequences

2.5 What's the news?

In this unit, you will:
- learn about the structure and features of a news report
- identify the writer's perspective and how it is presented
- write your own crime report.

What's the big idea?
Journalists write news reports to give their readers facts about events. Most news reports follow a similar structure in order to give the reader a summary of important information. Some journalists write more than just facts and give their perspective on the news.

Many journalists try to present information in a balanced, **objective** way, so the reader can form their own opinions about events. Other journalists write in a more **subjective** way, expressing their perspective in a more **sensationalist** style, to create an emotional reaction in their readers.

In this unit, you will learn about how to structure a news report and also have the opportunity to write your own news report about a crime, expressing your own perspective about events.

🔑 Key terms
objective not influenced by personal feeling or opinion

sensationalist presented in a deliberate way to stir up excitement and interest

subjective influenced by personal feeling or opinion

⚙ Activity 1

a What features would you expect to see in a news article?

b What do you already know about how journalists write newspaper articles?

c What techniques would you expect to see in news reporting?

d What different attitudes might journalists writing about crime express?

The news report opposite was published in the *Express* Online in May 2019. It focuses on a crime that was committed when a group of young people broke into a local school and destroyed a model railway exhibition.

88

Grown men in tears as DISGUSTING yobs DESTROY beloved model railway exhibition for fun

MINDLESS YOBS left grown men in tears and caused thousands of pounds of damage when they smashed up a model railway exhibition leaving its members heartbroken.

By **LAURA MOWAT** 09:40, Mon, May 20, 2019

The scumbags rampaged through a school hall where model rail enthusiasts had lovingly prepared the exhibition to showcase their work. Most of the exhibits - miniaturised versions of real railways - had taken years of craftsmanship, dedication and skill to create.

Those years of dedication were destroyed in minutes as the vandals left the room in tatters.

The horrific rampage led to the cancellation of the Market Deeping Model Railway Club's show in Stamford, Lincs.

A crowdfunding page raising funds for the group has already raised more than £50,000.

Four youths have been arrested on suspicion of burglary and criminal damage and have been released on **conditional bail**.

Club chairman, Peter Davies, said the display had taken hours to prepare and included some exhibitions which were the 'life's work' of some members.

The exhibition was expected to attract between 500 to 600 people from across the country and was due to begin on Saturday.

Peter Davies, 70, of Market Deeping, Lincolnshire, said: "We are devastated and distraught.

"It's heartbreaking. There were grown men there in tears because of what had been done, and I admit I was one of them.

"Can you imagine your life's work wrecked? One guy spent 25 years on his work and it's wrecked, it's just horrendous. They left it like a bomb site.

"We had to abandon the whole thing because it was scene of total devastation.

"We will never have the time to build the sort of layouts again, that's where the anger comes from. Some of the models were irreplaceable.

"Work that had taken many years to complete was totally destroyed.

"There were many different models of **locomotives** across the hall that were smashed, trodden and kicked about.

"Tables and layouts were overturned, dioramas were trashed, it was total devastation and destruction.

"There was no plan it was mindless. I have no idea why someone would do this.

"The damage will top tens of thousands of pounds but it will never recompense the time, skill and love that went into making those models, you can't compensate that.

"People have spent their lives building a model and then to see it trashed, there is no human emotion you can explain - just total despair.

"But we've had support from all over the world - as far away as New Zealand and we will rise back from this'."

---

rampage – violent and uncontrollable behaviour

conditional bail – when someone who is accused of committing a crime is allowed to wait for their court case outside of prison, if they follow a set of rules

locomotive – railway engine

2: Crime and consequences

⭐ Boosting your vocabulary

Writers choose their words carefully. The activity below focuses on some key vocabulary in the source text, which has been highlighted on page 89.

Activity 2

a The writer uses four different nouns to describe the people who committed the crime:

> youths   yobs   scumbags   vandals

   i What are the connotations of these words?

   For example, 'youths' means young people and has the connotation of teenagers who don't have a sense of responsibility or do not have respect for the rules.

   ii Why do you think the writer chose these words?

b The victims of the crime are described as 'devastated' and 'distraught'. What other synonyms could the writer have used to describe how the crime has affected them?

c What **adjectives** would you use to describe the writer's tone in this article? You may wish to choose from the words below or think of your own. Explain your choice, using evidence from the text.

> furious   sad   angry   surprised
>
> outraged   annoyed   resentful   vengeful

🔑 Key terms

adjective a word that describes a noun

byline a line at the beginning or end of a newspaper or magazine article that gives the writer's name

empathy the ability to understand and share in someone else's feelings

headline the title of a news article printed in large letters

purpose the reason that a text is written

standfirst a sentence or two beneath a headline, but before the main body of an article, which introduces what follows

💡 Building your knowledge

A newspaper report always starts with a **headline** at the top, to gain the reader's attention. A good headline summarises what the report is about, giving enough information to get the reader interested but leaving out enough details to make the reader want to find out more.

The headline is usually followed by a **standfirst**, which gives the main facts of the story but no great detail, so the reader needs to keep reading to be properly informed.

The **byline** tells the reader who wrote the article.

Activity 3

a Identify the following features in the source text:
   i headline   ii standfirst   iii byline

b Explain how the first two fulfil their **purpose** and draw the reader into the text.

Most newspaper reports follow a set structure because readers might not want to read the whole of the article. The structure of a news report can be presented in a diagram like the one opposite.

When writers report on crime for newspapers it is important that they include factual information about *what* has happened, *where*, *when*, *who* was involved and *why* the crime took place. These are called the 5 Ws, but the information also needs to include an H – *how* the action took place.

A news report may also include statistics to give the reader an insight into the scale of the crime and its effects. Witness statements – quotations from people at the scene of the crime – may be included to give the reader insight into the effect of the crime on people and the longer-term consequences. This focus on individuals gives the news article human interest and enables the reader to feel more **empathy** for people affected by the crime.

Most important information
5 Ws and H
What readers MUST know

More details
Important and unique details, but the reader will not be lost without them

Conclusion
Information that is helpful to have, but not critical

Activity 4

Re-read the extract.

a What are the 5 Ws and the H for this crime?

b Re-read the paragraph above. What additional features does the writer include in the article that are less important but still of interest to the reader?

2: Crime and consequences

Activity 5

Create a plan to write your own crime report about a theft. You could complete a table like the one below.

What has been stolen?	
Where was it stolen from?	
When was it stolen?	
Who stole it? Who is the victim?	
Why was it stolen?	
How was it stolen?	

The writer of the crime report on page 89 expresses their view of the crime in the **emotive language** they use and the sensationalist tone created by the descriptions and quotations.

Activity 6

a Rewrite the headline and standfirst of the report in a more objective style, taking out any emotive language and including only facts.

b **Compare** the two openings. Which do you think has most appeal to readers? Explain your answer carefully.

Key terms

compare judge how two or more things are similar and different

emotive language word choices that create a strong emotional reaction in the reader

Stretch yourself

A student who read the report said: 'The report is subjective and sensationalist. For that reason I don't think it's very reliable.' To what extent do you agree?

2.5: What's the news?

Putting it all together

Activity 7

Using the knowledge you have gained about the structure and features of news reports, you are now going to write your own crime report. Follow the steps below.

Step 1: Look back at the plan you made for your crime report. Think carefully about whether you are going to write an objective, factual crime report, or a sensationalist report. Write a headline and standfirst for your article.

Step 2: Decide what other features you will include in your crime report, apart from the 5 Ws and H. You may wish to consider:
- statistics
- witness statements
- emotive language
- a conclusion that looks at the consequences of the crime, including the fate of the criminals.

Step 3: Create a word bank of vocabulary that you could use in your crime report.

Step 4: Write a first draft of your crime report.

Step 5: Check your work (or your partner's work). The questions below might be helpful.
- Is the most important information at the start of the report?
- Are the headline and standfirst likely to grab the reader's attention?
- Is there a consistent tone in the report? For example, is the writer's attitude and perspective expressed clearly throughout?
- Are there any details that add human interest to the report?
- What do you think the report's purpose is? For example, is it mainly to inform the reader of events, or entertain them and stir up emotions? Does it succeed?

Step 6: Write a final draft of your crime report using the feedback from your partner or your own reflections on your first draft.

2: Crime and consequences

2.6 What is figurative language?

In this unit, you will:
- learn to identify and consider the effects of figurative language
- explore how figurative language can be used to express a perspective
- evaluate the effects of figurative language in a poem.

What's the big idea?

Writers use figurative language as a way to present ideas to the reader in an imaginative, interesting way. Instead of just writing about things in a literal way, they conjure up pictures and patterns of sound in the reader's mind, provoking more powerful or more subtle ideas and connotations.

In this unit, you will look at how poets use **figurative language** to give the reader an insight into the mind of two narrators – both of whom are guilty of committing a crime.

Activity 1

a What figurative language techniques do you already know about? Note your ideas in a mind map, giving a definition and example for each. It might start like the one below.

- simile
- **figurative language**
- personification
  - definition: representing something non-human as having human characteristics, e.g. the stars winked

b What can make analysing figurative language difficult? How can you overcome this challenge?

Key terms

figurative language words or phrases with a meaning that is different from the literal meaning

monologue a speech by one character

94

2.6: What is figurative language?

'Stealing' is a poem by Carol Ann Duffy. It is a **monologue**, written from the point of view of a thief.

While you are reading, think about:
- who the narrator (speaker) is
- what sort of person the narrator is. How do you know?
- what you think the poet wants us to think about this character.

'Stealing' by Carol Ann Duffy

The most unusual thing I ever stole? A snowman.
Midnight. He looked magnificent; a tall, white **mute**
beneath the winter moon. I wanted him, a mate
with a mind as cold as the slice of ice
5   within my own brain. I started with the head.

Better off dead than giving in, not taking
what you want. He weighed a ton; his **torso**,
frozen stiff, hugged to my chest, a fierce chill
piercing my gut. Part of the thrill was knowing
10 that children would cry in the morning. Life's tough.

Sometimes I steal things I don't need. I **joy-ride** cars
to nowhere, break into houses just to have a look.
I'm a mucky ghost, leave a mess, maybe pinch a camera.
I watch my gloved hand twisting the doorknob.
15 A stranger's bedroom. Mirrors. I sigh like this – Aah.

It took some time. **Reassembled** in the yard,
he didn't look the same. I took a run
and booted him. Again. Again. My breath ripped out
in rags. It seems daft now. Then I was standing
20 alone among lumps of snow, sick of the world.

Boredom. Mostly I'm so bored I could eat myself.
One time, I stole a guitar and thought I might
learn to play. I nicked a **bust** of Shakespeare once,
flogged it, but the snowman was the strangest.
25 You don't understand a word I'm saying, do you?

---

mute – outdated term for someone who doesn't speak
torso – the stomach and chest of a person
joy-ride – drive dangerously in a stolen vehicle
reassembled – put back together
bust – a sculpture of a person's head, shoulders and chest
flogged – sold

2: Crime and consequences

⭐ Boosting your vocabulary

Writers choose their words carefully. The activity below focuses on some key vocabulary in the source text, which has been highlighted on page 95.

Activity 2

a Find the different synonyms the writer uses for 'steal', 'stole' or 'stealing'.

b Why do you think the poet uses so many synonyms? Select one idea from the list below and explain why you think this.
   - For variety (Why is this important?)
   - To make stealing seem less serious (Why would the poet want to do this?)
   - To emphasise how often the character steals (Why would the poet want to do this?)

c The character talks about the 'thrill' they feel when they steal, knowing it will upset children. What word does the poet use later in the poem which could be considered the antonym of 'thrill'? Explain your answer carefully.

d At the end of the fourth **stanza**, the character is standing 'alone'. What are the connotations of the word 'alone'? Why do you think this might be important?

e What examples of **colloquial language** can you find in this text? Why do you think the writer chose to use this type of language?

✅ Tip

Remember that an antonym means the opposite, so you are looking for a word that describes a mood or state of mind that is far from thrilled.

🗝 Key terms

alliteration using the same letter or sound at the beginning of several words for special effect

colloquial language informal words or phrases that are suitable for ordinary conversation, rather than formal speech or writing

onomatopoeia words that imitate or suggest what they stand for, e.g. *cuckoo*, *sizzle*

repetition using the same word or phrase more than once

stanza a group of lines in a poem with a line space before and after it

Activity 3

a What do you learn about the narrator in this poem? Note any 'facts' you can find about them.

b What can you infer about the character and how they feel about their life?

2.6: What is figurative language?

💡 Building your knowledge

Writers use figurative language to create an engaging variety of images in the reader's mind. The images might involve comparisons such as **similes** and metaphors, which give additional ideas about the **subject**. Figurative language can also trigger a range of sensations in the reader. The sensations might arise from different patterns of sound, such as **repetition**, **alliteration** and **onomatopoeia**. These patterns might emphasise certain words, reinforce images or convey feelings to the reader.

In the poem 'Stealing' the poet uses figurative language to help express the perspective of the criminal, and also to reveal something about their character. The poet uses other language techniques, such as **rhetorical questions**, and colloquial language to help make the perspective and character really clear for the reader.

🔑 Key terms

rhetorical question a question asked for dramatic effect and not intended to get an answer

simile a comparison of one thing to another, using *as* or *like*, e.g. *He swam like a fish*

subject the person or thing that does the verb, e.g. *the boy* eats, *tigers* prowl, *the building* exists

Activity 4

Complete a table like the one below. The first row has been completed for you.

a Find an example of each language technique in the poem.
b Note what effect it creates for the reader.
c Note what it reveals about the character of the narrator.
d Add at least one more row to your table, analysing another language technique that the poet uses.

Technique	Evidence	Effect	What this reveals about the character
Imagery	'a fierce chill / piercing my gut'	This helps the reader to imagine how much the narrator felt the cold – 'fierce' and 'piercing' suggest that the cold is intimidating and painful.	This suggests that they really want to steal the snowman because they are undergoing pain to do so.
Simile			
Metaphor			
Repetition			
Rhetorical question			
Colloquial language			

2: Crime and consequences

Activity 5

A student who read 'Stealing' said: 'I actually feel sorry for the thief – it's obvious they haven't got anything else to do and that's why they steal. I think they're lonely too.'

To what extent do you agree?

Consider:
- how the author makes you feel towards the thief
- what techniques the author uses to make you feel this way
- what you can infer about what sort of person the thief is
- whether or not you agree that the thief is lonely.

Putting it all together

The poem below is another dramatic monologue about someone feeling guilty as a consequence of committing a crime. As you read, think carefully about the difference in attitude conveyed by this narrator, compared with the narrator of 'Stealing'.

'Guilty Conscience' by Sagar Garg

Silence falls over me at the night,
covers me in a heavy blanket of darkness and guilt.
I try and **exhale** my **sins** but they **smother** me back
as I am forced to breathe them back in.
5　The hands on the clock taunt me with their sound,
acknowledging my lack of sleep.
My vision is blurred. My judgement is **compromised**.
Nothing can undo what I have done.
The rain will not wash away my guilty conscience.
10　The sun will not brighten my inner darkness.
It will only serve to **expose** the truth
when the shadows **dissipate** and **unearth** my face.
Denial is no longer an option, it never was…

---

guilty conscience – a bad feeling of regret caused by knowing that you have done something wrong
exhale – breathe out
sin – the breaking of a moral or religious law

smother – to cover something thickly
compromised – damaged
expose / unearth – reveal
dissipate – reduce or disappear
denial – refusal to accept something

2.6: What is figurative language?

Activity 6

a What does the narrator in this poem feel about the crimes they have committed? How do you know?

b How is the narrator in this poem similar or different to the narrator in 'Stealing'?

c What figurative language techniques can you identify and what effects do they create for the reader?

Activity 7

> A student who read 'Guilty Conscience' said: 'The speaker in this poem regrets their actions and feels guilty for what they have done. I feel sympathy for the speaker because they are truly sorry.' To what extent do you agree?

a Make some brief notes about:
   - how the writer makes you feel towards the narrator
   - what techniques the writer uses to make you feel this way
   - what you have inferred about what sort of person the narrator is
   - whether or not you agree they are sorry.

b Write a full response, using your notes and the model below to help you.

Step 1: Explain how you feel about the speaker: *The author presents the speaker as… This makes me feel they are…*

Step 2: Identify a technique the poet uses and give evidence from the text: *The author uses a metaphor, 'a heavy blanket of darkness and guilt'…*

Step 3: Explore the impact of the technique: *This makes the reader feel…*

Explore the implicit meaning of the evidence used: *This could suggest…*

Step 4: Evaluate to what extent you agree with the statement: *This is effective in making me feel sorry for the speaker because…*

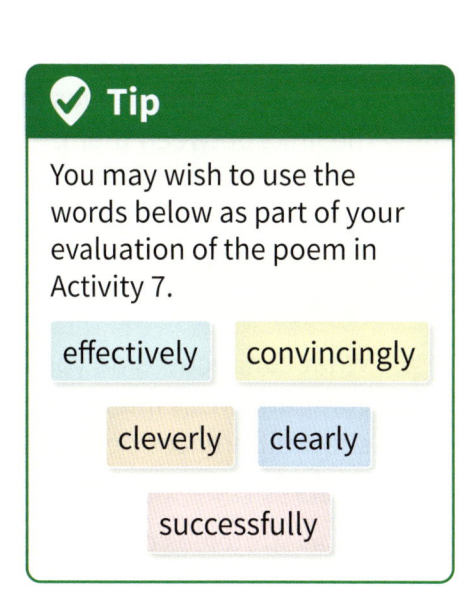

Tip

You may wish to use the words below as part of your evaluation of the poem in Activity 7.

effectively   convincingly   cleverly   clearly   successfully

2: Crime and consequences

2.7 What's the difference?

In this unit, you will:
- learn to compare texts
- summarise and synthesise the main points of two texts
- compare how writers present their perspectives.

What's the big idea?
It is important to be able to compare texts, particularly on the same subject, so that we can explore the similarities and differences between them. This includes both *what* the writers are saying and *how* they are saying it. In order to make a clear comparison, we have to identify and synthesise the main points of the texts, then consider how the writers present their perspectives.

In this unit, you will read two accounts of prison life written by criminals who were imprisoned as a consequence of their alleged crimes. Michael Romero was convicted in America for bank robbery; Florence Maybrick was an American who was convicted of murdering her husband while living in England. The two accounts were written more than 100 years apart. A comparison can help the reader to understand how the experience of being in prison has changed over time – and what aspects remain the same.

To compare texts, first we need to be able to identify the main points of each and summarise them. We can then analyse similarities and differences using **connectives** (**adverbials** and **conjunctions**) to show the links between them.

Activity 1

a What connectives do you know that you can use to make comparisons? Find three to show similarities and three to show differences between two ideas. Here are two to get you started. *in the same way, in contrast.*

b What strategies can you use to find the main points in a text?

c What do you already know about different ways writers might put across their perspective?

Key terms

adverbial a word or phrase that explains how, where or when something happened, or shows how ideas relate to one another

conjunction a linking word, e.g. *if, and, but*

connective a general term for a word or phrase that helps link information

2.7: What's the difference?

Now read the two accounts of prison life. As you read these texts, think about:
- when each text was written and by whom. How might this affect the writer's perspective?
- what techniques the writers use to present their perspective
- what is similar or different about their experiences.

Text A was written in 2012.

Text A: *A Day in the Life of a Prisoner* by Michael Romero

We are confined to one cellblock and not allowed in any other. From our cellblock we can go to the yard, the **mess hall**, or our job. Movements are allowed hourly during a ten-minute period. Many of us spend our free time in the yard, which is a precious place indeed. In the yard, we have handball courts, tennis courts, weights, basketball, volleyball, a running track, green grass, and miles and
5 miles of blue sky and fresh air. It's the place where we play, shaking off the dust, disease, and gloom of the cage.

A man with an afternoon job may come to spend his mornings on the yard, afternoons at work, and his evenings studying in his cell. This routine is as certain to him as the years he must do.

[...]

Back in the cellblock, some of us remove our running shoes and go back to bed, sleeping all day
10 and tossing and turning all night. Others sit in the stuffy cellblock and watch the rays of sunshine filtering through the iron security screens on the windows.

Taking away the yard spoils our routine and unbalances our body clocks. Tempers begin to go bad; we snap at each other like too many rats crammed into a cardboard box; hating becomes second nature.

[...]

No matter how we approach the issue **intellectually**, it doesn't dampen the rage we acquire from
15 being packed in gloomy cages while there is blue sky and sunshine just beyond the wall. We have to share this place down to our germs. If one gets the flu, we all get it.

When our routines are disrupted, chaos is once again among us. The future seems fragmented, uncertain. A strange type of **resolve** takes hold among the convicts; should our keepers choose to deal in pain, chaos, and destruction, we will try to give them a good game. After all, we invented it.

mess hall – dining room
intellectually – with careful thinking
resolve – firm decision

2: Crime and consequences

Text B was published in 1904.

Text B: *My Fifteen Lost Years* by Florence Maybrick

No one can realise the horror of **solitary confinement** who has not experienced it.

Here is one day's routine: It is six o'clock; I arise and dress in the dark; I put up my hammock and
5   wait for breakfast. I hear the ward officer in the gallery outside. I take a tin plate and a tin mug in my hands and stand before the cell door.

Presently the door opens; a brown, whole-meal, six-ounce loaf is placed upon the plate; the tin
10   mug is taken, and three-quarters of a pint of **gruel** is measured in my presence, when the mug is handed back in silence, and the door is closed and locked. After I have taken a few mouthfuls of bread I begin to scrub my cell.

15   A bell rings and my door is again unlocked. No word is spoken, because I know exactly what to do. I leave my cell and fall into single file, three paces in the rear of my nearest fellow convict. All of us are alike in knowing what we have to do,
20   and we march away silently to **Divine service**. We are criminals under punishment, and **our keepers** march us like cattle to the worship of God. [...]

Chapel over, I returned directly to my cell, for I was in solitary confinement, and might not enjoy
25   the privilege of working in company with my prison **companions**.

---

solitary – alone or single
gruel – a watered-down version of porridge/oatmeal
Divine service – a Christian church service
our keepers – prison officers
companions – people you spend time with

❓ Did you know?

Despite being in prison for 15 years, Florence Maybrick was later cleared of poisoning her husband. Her case was explored in many **non-fiction** books and inspired many fiction novels.

🔑 Key term

non-fiction real events or factual information

2.7: What's the difference?

⭐ Boosting your vocabulary

Writers choose their words carefully. The activity below focuses on some key vocabulary in the source texts, which has been highlighted on pages 101 and 102.

Activity 2

a   Both writers use the word 'routine' in their texts. This word comes from the Old French word *rute*, meaning road.

   i   Explain the meaning of the word 'routine' and give some examples from both texts.

   ii Why do you think the word 'routine' developed from the idea of a road? Explain your answer carefully.

b   Romero talks about how the prisoners are 'confined' and Maybrick refers to her 'confinement'. These words have Latin origins, linked to *con* (together) and *finis* (limits).

   i   Complete a Frayer model diagram like the one below to explore the meaning and connotations of the word 'confinement'.

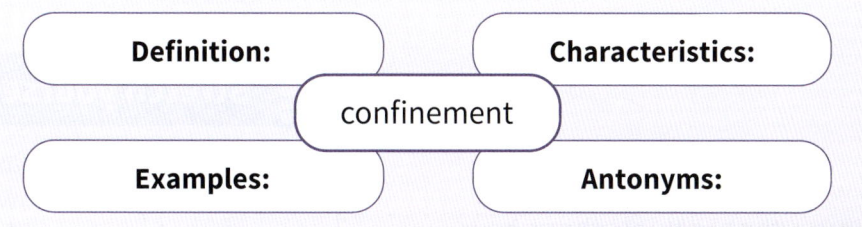

   Definition: **Characteristics:**
               confinement
   Examples: **Antonyms:**

   ii Romero uses the images of a 'box' and a 'cage' to convey his feelings about his confinement. Find them in the text. Explain the connotations of these words and images and how they help the reader to understand Romero's perspective.

c   Find the following words and phrases in Romero's account:

   chaos   fragmented   rage   destruction   tossing and turning

   What impression do they create for the reader about Romero's attitude towards life in prison?

d   How does Romero describe life outside in the yard compared to life inside the prison? How does this make the reader feel towards Romero?

e   Maybrick uses the words 'solitary' and 'silence' in her description of prison life. Explain how these convey a negative perspective of prison life in her account.

2: Crime and consequences

Building your knowledge

Synthesising is one way of considering how we have understood a text or texts. It helps us to pick out the main points and draw together more than one idea or perspective. When we synthesise it's important to use evidence from the text, but also to infer additional, less obvious details, showing a deeper level of understanding of the text.

> **Key term**
>
> **synthesise** to combine separate parts into something new

Activity 3

> What do both writers show the reader about what life is like in prison? What are the similarities and differences between their experiences?

Complete a Venn diagram like the one opposite. Consider each writer's experience in prison and how they feel about it.

- Anything that is the same for both writers should go in the overlapping middle section of the diagram.
- Anything that is different should go in the circle for each individual text.

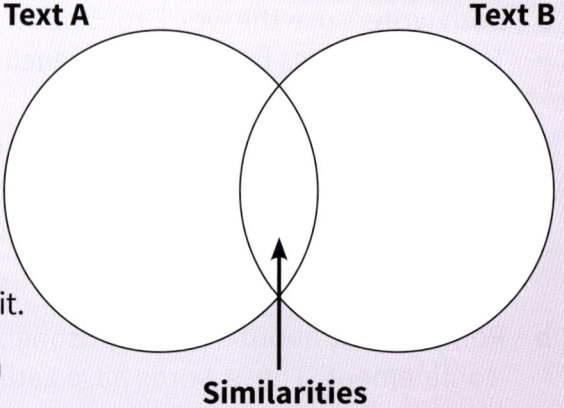

Text A   Text B

↑ Similarities

Activity 4

Now that you have identified *what* the writers are sharing about their experiences, it is important to think about *how* they share it.

a Look back at your Venn diagram and both texts. Identify some of the language techniques the writers have used to convey prison life. Think about how the writers have used metaphors, exaggeration, emotive language and similes.

b Now consider *how* these techniques help the writers to put across their perspective. For each language technique you have identified, make a note of:

- what the writer is telling us about life in prison
- what we can infer about how they feel about life in prison
- how the technique helps the reader to imagine how the writer feels
- why the writer has used this technique.

> **↑ Stretch yourself**
>
> Identify words and phrases that implicitly show how the writers feel about life in prison. For example:
>
> > Maybrick frequently refers to the silence that is enforced. The repetition suggests she finds it boring and difficult to live without being able to talk to anyone.

2.7: What's the difference?

Putting it all together

Activity 5

a Read the question below.

> Compare how the writers of Text A and Text B present their perspectives of their experiences in prison.

Plan your response to the question, considering each of these points in turn:
- *what* their perspective and attitude is towards their prison experience
- *how* they use different language techniques to communicate their perspective
- *why* they use these techniques. How do they impact on the reader?

b Read this extract from one student's answer and the teacher's comments.

> In Text A, Romero thinks it is a good thing that prison is very ordered and controlled, whereas in Text B, Maybrick thinks life in prison is horrible because of the control and order. Romero uses a simile, 'we snap at each other like too many rats crammed into a cardboard box'. This shows that when the order and routine are taken away the prisoners become unhappy. This helps the reader to imagine how difficult life is in prison. In contrast, Maybrick uses the simile 'our keepers march us like cattle'. This shows she thinks the routine is horrible and finds it is like being treated like an animal.

I like the way you make a really clear point about how the writers feel about prison and compare both texts using the adverbial 'whereas'. You have selected great quotations to support your idea and explained what the quotations imply about the writers' experiences of prison. It would be even better if you could explore how these quotations make the reader feel for the writers.

c Using your notes, and bearing in mind the teacher's comments, write your own response in full.

105

2: Crime and consequences

2.8 Can a text change your mind?

In this unit, you will:
- learn to identify methods used to communicate attitudes and perspectives
- explore techniques to make your perspective persuasive
- write and present a contribution to a debate.

What's the big idea?

In this unit, you will look at how a writer can present a strong personal perspective in an article about juvenile crime. You will explore some of the persuasive devices the writer uses to convince the reader that their perspective is right, such as the use of anecdotes and statistics. You will have the opportunity to use these devices yourself in a debate about young people and crime.

Activity 1

a Think of a time you have tried to persuade someone to agree with your point of view. What was challenging about it? How did you persuade them?

b What other **persuasive** language techniques do you know about? Note down your ideas on a mind map, giving definitions and examples.

Key terms

editorial a newspaper article expressing a writer's opinion

juvenile linked to young people

persuasive making you want to do or believe something

The following **editorial** about **juvenile** crime was published in the *Independent* newspaper in 2014. An editorial usually comments on a recent event or current social issue. Why do you think an editorial might have persuasive features?

Who should get credit for declining youth crime?
Young people, of course

They are responsible for a record drop in the crime rate, so we should stop demonising them

by Ally Fog

Some teenagers tried to rob me the other evening. I was walking my dog on an isolated stretch of the Manchester Cycleway between the run-down neighbourhoods of Gorton and Levenshulme around dusk.

A gang of about half a dozen boys and girls, aged around 15 and sporting urban uniform tracksuit bottoms and hoodies came towards me.

They took one look at my dog, crouched down, and said something like: "Oo look atchoo! What a gorgeous liddle puppy wuppy, yesh you are. I'm going to steal you and take you home with me. Come on, come with me doggie…"

They then danced off in the opposite direction, with my **pliant** little mutt skipping merrily after them. I let them escape a few yards before calling him to me. As he obediently galloped back, the young bandits gave some **melodramatic** wails, "No! Come back!" then we all laughed, waved, and went our separate ways.

Not exactly **Eden Lake**, I know. Nonetheless, this little non-event illustrates a stark but **seldom-noted** truth about our young people. They are remarkably **law-abiding**.

The latest statistics from the Ministry of Justice show that the number of people involved with the criminal justice system is at the lowest level since records began in 1970, and the drop is very largely driven by young people.

In 2007 there were 126,500 **prosecutions** of juveniles, in 2013 there were 48,000. Young people accounted for only 3% of **defendants** prosecuted in 2013 compared to 7% in 2007.

[…]

It has long been said that the devil makes work for idle hands, and a lot of juvenile delinquency has always been a product of boredom. It may simply be the case that when young people have a choice of smartphone, tablet and games console in front of them, they feel less need to […] smash up a bus shelter.

It's true, but having said that, this explanation still seems a **trifle churlish**. As a society we have few hesitations in laying the blame on our young people when things go badly. But we should be equally quick to offer applause when things go right.

The inescapable truth is that young people today are less criminal, less violent, less dangerous than at any time in recent memory, and **credit** for that goes not to Sony, Apple or Microsoft, but to young people themselves.

---

pliant – easily influenced
melodramatic – over the top/exaggerated
Eden Lake – a horror film about delinquent teenagers
seldom-noted – not often mentioned
law-abiding – obedient to the law

prosecutions – official accusations of law-breaking
defendants – people accused of committing a crime in court
trifle churlish – little bit rude
credit – recognition or praise

2: Crime and consequences

⭐ Boosting your vocabulary

Writers choose their words carefully. The activity below focuses on some key vocabulary in the source text, which has been highlighted on page 107.

Activity 2

a   The word 'demon' can mean an evil spirit or a cruel, destructive person.
   i   What does it mean to 'demonise' someone?
   ii How might it feel to be 'demonised'? Think of an example when this has happened to you or someone you know.
   iii What synonyms can you think of for the word 'demonised'?

b   What sort of behaviours or acts could be classed as 'delinquent'? Why do you think young people or 'juveniles' are often called 'delinquent'?

c   The prefix 'de-' is used in lots of words in this article. This prefix is inherited from French and Latin, where it usually means 'down', 'off' or 'away'. In English, the prefix 'de-' can mean lots of things.
   i   Find all the words with the prefix 'de-' in the article.
   ii Think of a word that uses the prefix 'de-' to show each of the following:
       • to undo an action, for example 'defrost'
       • to make less, for example 'decline'.

Activity 3

a   What is the writer's perspective on young people? How do you know?
b   What persuasive techniques can you identify that the writer uses to persuade the reader that his perspective is correct?
c   Do you agree with the writer's perspective? Why or why not?
d   With a partner or in small groups, talk about this statement:

> 'Adults have a really poor opinion of teenagers. If they spent more time talking to us they'd realise we're not causing problems.'

Give your view of this statement (whether you agree or disagree with it), including your reasons. Listen carefully to other people's points of view.

2.8: Can a text change your mind?

Building your knowledge

In an editorial, the writer is generally expressing their view on a recent event or a current issue and they want to persuade the reader to agree with their perspective. There are many language techniques that writers can use that can encourage the reader to agree with them. For example, an **anecdote** can entertain the reader and also illustrate a point that the writer wants to make.

Another device that writers often use to emphasise their point and make it more memorable is **tricolon**. Using this structure is another effective way of presenting clear information and images for the reader, encouraging them to share the writer's perspective.

Statistics can help to persuade a reader because they offer facts and evidence. The vocabulary that writers use can also help to persuade readers to agree with their perspective. Words that create impact or appeal to a reader's emotions are likely to be more persuasive than less memorable vocabulary.

> **Key terms**
>
> **anecdote** a short or entertaining story about real people or events
>
> **tricolon** a pattern of three words or phrases grouped together to be memorable and have impact

Activity 4

a   Complete a table like the one below. The first row has been completed for you.

Technique	Evidence	Impact
Statistic	Only 3% of defendants prosecuted in 2013 were juveniles, compared to 7% in 2007.	This statistic supports the writer's perspective that juvenile crime is decreasing. The use of the statistic makes the reader trust what is being said and more likely to agree with the perspective because it has been researched.
Anecdote		
Opinion		
Tricolon		
Emotive language		

b   Which persuasive technique do you think is most effective in the source text and why?

Stretch yourself

Identify another persuasive technique that the writer uses in the source text. Add it to your table and explain the impact it has on the reader.

2: Crime and consequences

We see persuasive techniques in writing, but we can also hear them in speeches, for example speeches made by lawyers or politicians.

You are going to practise developing a persuasive speech to **debate** with your classmates.

Activity 5

a Think about what makes an effective speaker. What skills do you need?

b Look at the list of skills below. For each skill, rate yourself between 1 and 3. (1 = I'm confident I can do this well; 2 = I will have a go at this; 3 = I find this hard or I don't know how to do it.)
- Confidence
- **Fluency** (speaking with a smooth flow, without hesitating)
- Pace (speaking not too quickly or too slowly)
- Volume (not too loud or too quiet)
- **Gesture** (using your hands to help emphasise certain points)
- Body language (using posture to show your confidence)
- Eye contact (looking at the audience when you're speaking)
- Organisation (making sure your ideas are linked and go in an order that makes sense)

c Now order these skills from most to least important for you to be able to persuade your audience to agree with you.

d Explain the reason you have ranked your top skill the most important and your bottom skill the least important.

> **Key terms**
>
> **debate** to have a formal discussion in which opposite views on a subject are heard fairly
>
> **fluency** speaking with a smooth flow, without hesitating
>
> **gesture** using your hands to indicate meaning, e.g. to help emphasise certain points

Putting it all together

Using the skills you have learned in this unit, you are going to argue for or against the statement below in a debate.

> 'Young people today are out of control. They commit crime in our communities and ruin local areas for everyone else. They should be sent to prison for their crimes to make society safer for everyone.'

2.8: Can a text change your mind?

Activity 6

a Write a short paragraph for your contribution to the debate. In this paragraph you should make your perspective clear and use persuasive techniques to make the listeners agree with your point of view.

You may find it helpful to read this student example, and then the teacher's comments.

> I don't think it is fair to say young people today are out of control. 95% of young people don't commit crimes. This shows the majority of young people are law-abiding citizens, so this stereotype is very damaging, hurtful and wrong. It can make young people afraid to go out on the streets to see their friends because people will judge them without knowing them. If adults actually spoke to young people maybe they'd realise we're just like them.

You have a clear point of view and use a statistic, a tricolon and lots of emotive language. I like the way you have explained why you think and feel the way you do and offered a solution to the negative perspective.

b When you have written your paragraph, practise presenting it.

Check that:
- you have used persuasive devices
- your perspective is clear
- you are using the skills listed in Activity 5.

c Take part in a class debate. As well as presenting your own perspective, listen to and respond to the arguments put forward by other students.

d Review your performance in the debate.
- How did you feel about taking part in the debate?
- How did you overcome challenges?
- What strategies and skills did you use to help you write and present persuasively?
- When could you use these skills in the future?

✓ Tip

Remember that in a debate, everyone has the opportunity to express their views on the given statement. The debate ends with everyone voting on whether they agree or disagree with the given statement.

3 JOURNEYS AND DISCOVERIES

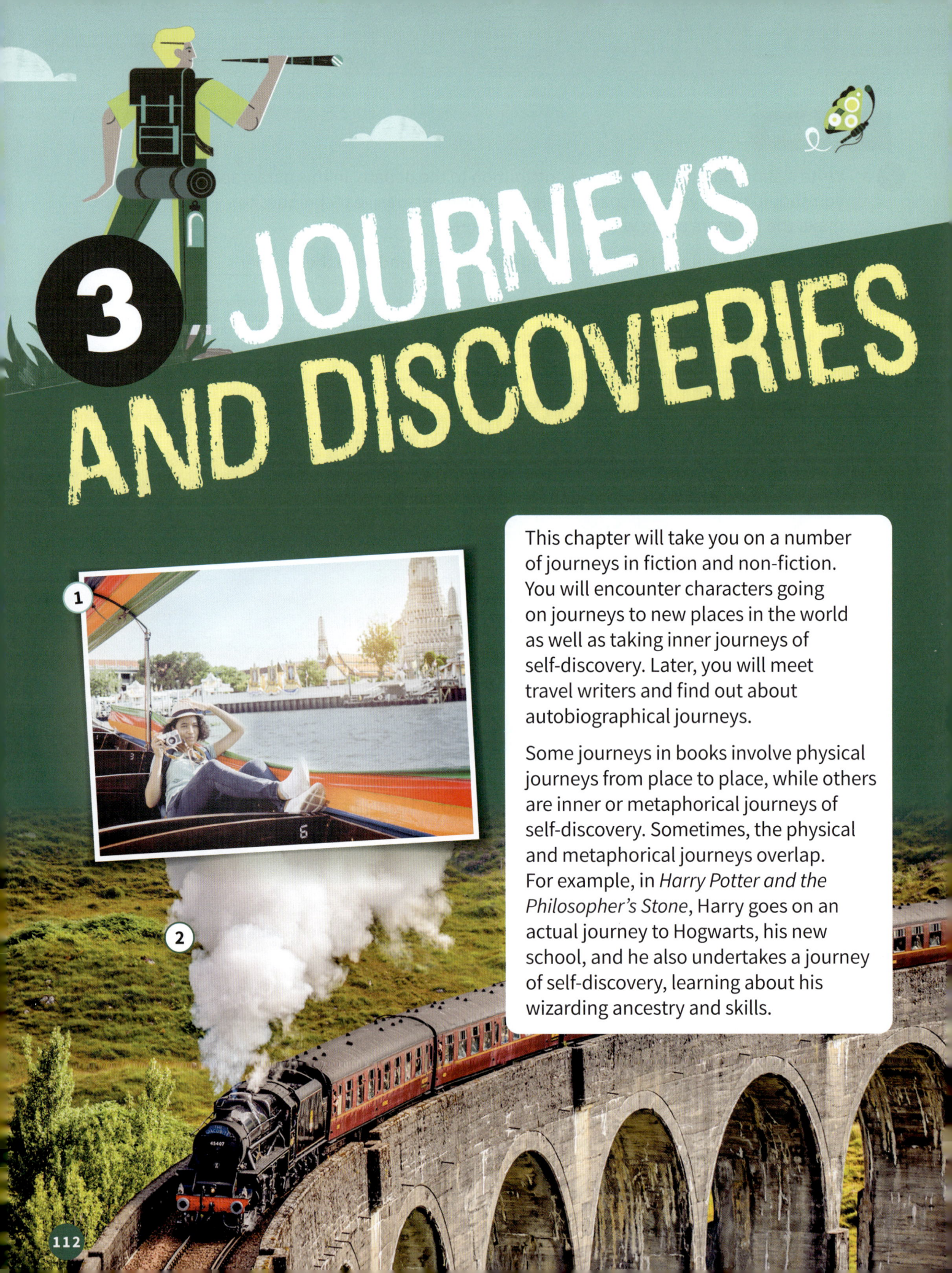

This chapter will take you on a number of journeys in fiction and non-fiction. You will encounter characters going on journeys to new places in the world as well as taking inner journeys of self-discovery. Later, you will meet travel writers and find out about autobiographical journeys.

Some journeys in books involve physical journeys from place to place, while others are inner or metaphorical journeys of self-discovery. Sometimes, the physical and metaphorical journeys overlap. For example, in *Harry Potter and the Philosopher's Stone*, Harry goes on an actual journey to Hogwarts, his new school, and he also undertakes a journey of self-discovery, learning about his wizarding ancestry and skills.

Use what you know

a   What is the longest journey you have ever been on? How did you travel? What were the ups and downs you experienced?

b   Have you ever had to travel somewhere you didn't want to go? What were the worst aspects of this? Were there any unexpected pleasures?

c   Does the idea of travel excite or worry you, and why? If you could travel anywhere in the world, where would you go, and why?

d   Look at the images of journeys on these pages. With your work partner, rank the journeys in different ways. For example, put the journeys in order from most boring to most exciting, most to least dangerous, and most expensive to cheapest.

Words you need to know

journeys, discovery, travel, jeopardy, challenge, expedition, quest, experience, sustainable

113

3: Journeys and discoveries

3 Learning overview

This learning overview will show you where the chapter will take you on your learning journey. Use it to help you plan your learning, monitor what you have learned and then evaluate your knowledge.

3.1 How do journeys create jeopardy? 116–121

Prepare
- What stories – from fairy tales, novels and films – do you know in which characters take dangerous journeys?

What I will learn
- How writers create a sense of danger.
- Some features of a coming-of-age story.

How I will learn
- Read an extract and identify the writer's choices.
- Write a commentary about the extract.

3.2 What is a quest? 122–127

Prepare
- What books have you read in which the characters went on a journey? Did the journey change them in any way?

What I will learn
- The main features of quest stories and other story types.
- How writers' choices impact on the reader.

How I will learn
- Read an extract and infer meaning from language choices.
- Write a first-person quest story.

3.3 Why start with a journey? 128–133

Prepare
- What films, books and plays do you know that begin with a journey?

What I will learn
- Key plot conventions.
- The effects of literary devices.

How I will learn
- Read an extract and identify the writer's techniques.
- Write about the extract in a formal, literary style.

3.4 How can poetry explore journeys? 134–139

Prepare
- What do you know about refugees from the news, people around you and prior reading?

What I will learn
- How texts are influenced by context.
- Poetic features and their effects.

How I will learn
- Read a poem and consider its context, meaning and impact.
- Perform a poem.

114

3.5 What is travel writing?
140–145

Prepare
- When you are extra observant, what do you notice around you on the journeys you make in your local area?

What I will learn
- The conventions of travel writing.
- The effects of features in travel writing.

How I will learn
- Read an extract and identify travel writing features.
- Write a non-fiction narrative based on a journey.

3.6 Why travel sustainably?
146–151

Prepare
- In your view, is it always a good thing to travel?

What I will learn
- Persuasive techniques and their effects.
- How to be successful when speaking in front of an audience.

How I will learn
- Read an extract and identify its persuasive features.
- Write and deliver a persuasive speech.

3.7 Why take a risk?
152–157

Prepare
- Have you ever chosen to do something dangerous, just for the thrill of it?

What I will learn
- The choices writers make when describing travel adventures.
- How to organise ideas into paragraphs.

How I will learn
- Read an extract and make links between the writer's words and feelings.
- Write an article for a travel website.

3.8 Can journeys tell stories?
158–163

Prepare
- What do you already know about segregation and the civil rights movement?

What I will learn
- The links between travel writing and autobiographical writing.
- How to analyse a literary text.

How I will learn
- Read an extract and respond to what it reveals about the writer's life.
- Write about the text, explaining its impact on readers, with evidence.

3: Journeys and discoveries

3.1 How do journeys create jeopardy?

In this unit, you will:
- learn how writers make deliberate choices to create a sense of danger
- explore the features of a 'coming-of-age' story
- analyse how a writer creates a sense of jeopardy in a text.

What's the big idea?

Jeopardy means danger of loss, harm or failure. Classic stories, such as fairy tales, are full of jeopardy – wicked witches, big bad wolves, threatening forests. Many authors look for ways to create this sense of danger, because it is the perfect way to draw readers in and make them want to turn the pages.

In this unit, you will read and respond to a **text** that creates a sense of threat and danger on a journey.

Activity 1

a Before you begin, think about the dangers and threats faced by **characters** in the stories below.

Jack and the Beanstalk   Jumanji   Harry Potter

Charlie and the Chocolate Factory   The Little Mermaid

Theseus and the Minotaur   Cinderella   Peter Pan   Star Wars

b Identify at least one more example of a story that features jeopardy.

In *The Body*, a novella by Stephen King published in 1982, 12-year-old Gordie LaChance and his three friends, Chris, Teddy and Vern, go on a long walk one hot summer day. They hope to find the body of a missing boy. The journey is full of jeopardy – a scary dog, a pond full of leeches and a terrifying railway bridge high over the Castle River that the boys must cross. Gordie is the **narrator**.

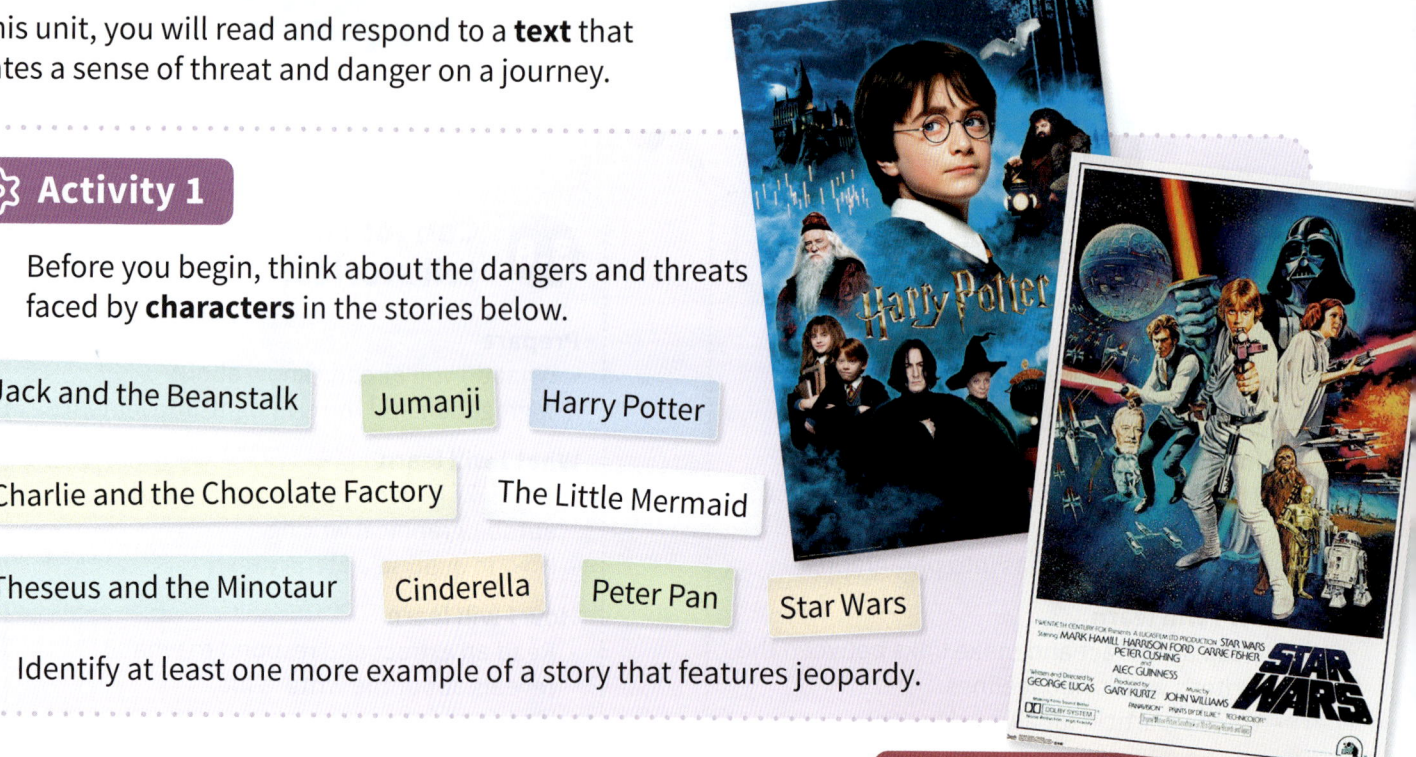

Key terms

character a person in a drama or story

narrator a person who tells a story, especially in a book, play or film

text any form of written material

3.1: How do journeys create jeopardy?

In this first extract, the boys see the dangerous bridge for the first time.

Extract 1: *The Body* by Stephen King

We were standing beside the tracks where the **cinders** sloped away towards the river's cut – the place where the embankment stopped and the **trestle** began. Looking down, I could see where the slope started to get steep. The cinders gave way to straggly, tough-looking bushes and slabs of grey rock. Further down there were a few stunted firs with exposed roots writhing their way out of fissures in the plates of rock; they seemed to be looking down at their own miserable reflections in the running water.

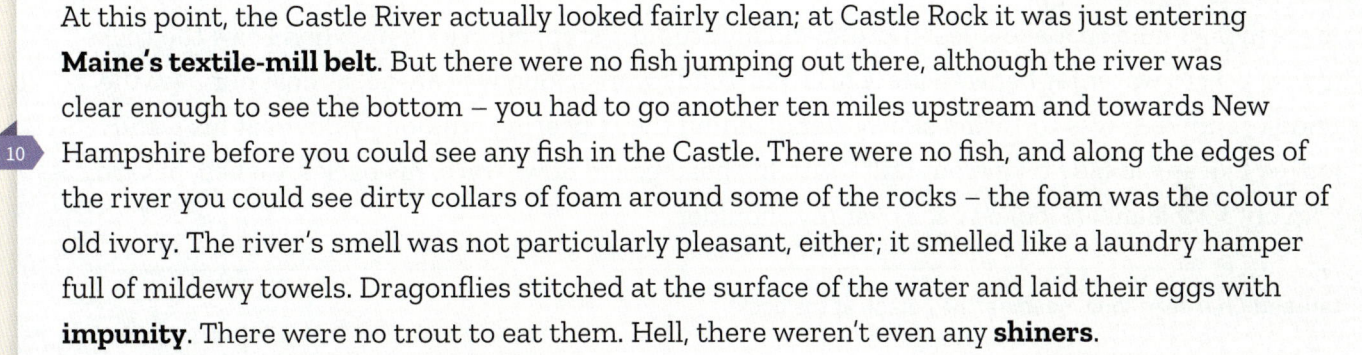

At this point, the Castle River actually looked fairly clean; at Castle Rock it was just entering **Maine's textile-mill belt**. But there were no fish jumping out there, although the river was clear enough to see the bottom – you had to go another ten miles upstream and towards New Hampshire before you could see any fish in the Castle. There were no fish, and along the edges of the river you could see dirty collars of foam around some of the rocks – the foam was the colour of old ivory. The river's smell was not particularly pleasant, either; it smelled like a laundry hamper full of mildewy towels. Dragonflies stitched at the surface of the water and laid their eggs with **impunity**. There were no trout to eat them. Hell, there weren't even any **shiners**.

"Man," Chris said softly.

"Come on," Teddy said in that brisk, arrogant way. "Let's go." He was already edging his way out, walking on the **six-by-fours** between the shining rails.

"Say," Vern said uneasily, "any of you guys know when the next train's due?"

We all shrugged.

I said: "There's the Route 136 bridge ..."

"Hey, come on, gimme a break!" Teddy cried. "That means walkin' five miles down the river on this side and then five miles back up on the other side ... it'll take us until dark! If we use the trestle, we can get to the same place in *ten minutes!*"

"But if a train comes, there's nowheres to go," Vern said. He wasn't looking at Teddy. He was looking down at the fast, bland river.

---

cinders – rocks like old pieces of coal near train tracks
trestle – the trestle bridge is made of short **six-by-fours** – planks of wood that are the railway sleepers or crossties – across a wooden frame

Maine's textile-mill belt – an area in North America where the main industry at the time was making textiles (fabrics)
impunity – free from punishment or danger
shiners – small, silvery fish

3: Journeys and discoveries

The boys discuss the risks of crossing. It's a quiet piece of single-track train line, but there is nowhere to go – apart from to fall into the river far below – if a train comes. In the next extract, they have made their decision.

Extract 2: *The Body* by Stephen King

We went out onto the trestle single-file: Chris first, then Teddy, then Vern, and me playing **tail-end Charlie** because I was the one who said dares go first. We walked on the platform crossties between the rails, and you had to look at your feet whether you were scared of heights or not. A misstep and you would go down to your crotch, probably with a broken ankle to pay.

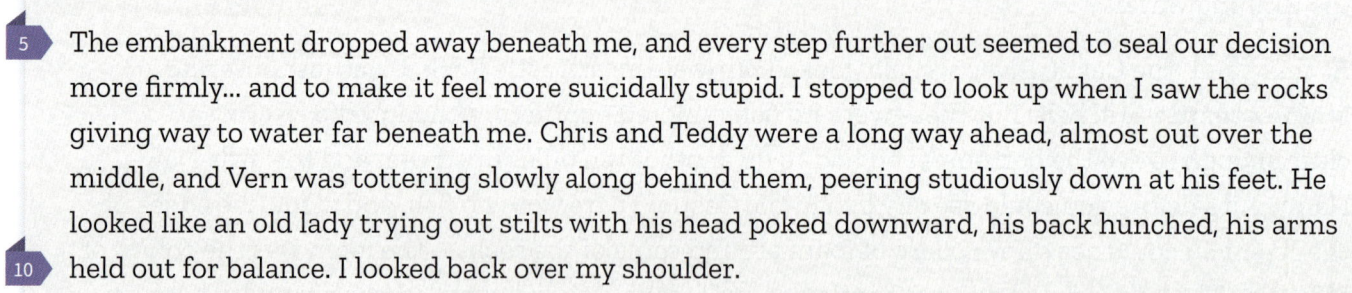

5 The embankment dropped away beneath me, and every step further out seemed to seal our decision more firmly... and to make it feel more suicidally stupid. I stopped to look up when I saw the rocks giving way to water far beneath me. Chris and Teddy were a long way ahead, almost out over the middle, and Vern was tottering slowly along behind them, peering studiously down at his feet. He looked like an old lady trying out stilts with his head poked downward, his back hunched, his arms 10 held out for balance. I looked back over my shoulder.

tail-end Charlie – slang meaning 'the person at the back'

Characters in quest narratives often have to face both physical and mental challenges along their journey; this is a key **convention** of the **genre**.

⭐ Boosting your vocabulary

Writers choose their words carefully. The activity below focuses on some key vocabulary in the source text, which has been highlighted on page 117.

Activity 2

a Re-read the description of the riverbanks under the bridge (lines 3–6) in extract 1. The vocabulary in these sentences creates a strong sense of danger. For each of the words below, choose the **synonym** that you think best creates a sense of danger.

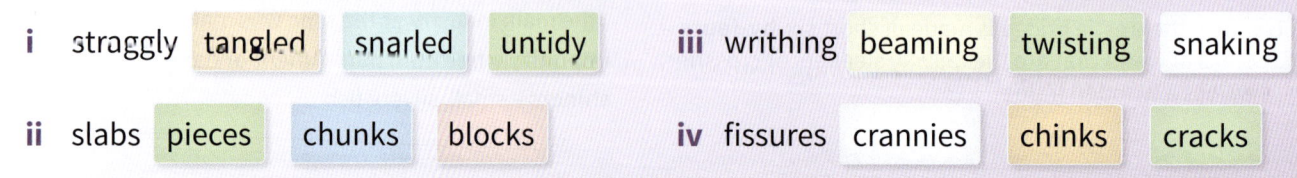

   i   straggly   tangled   snarled   untidy   iii writhing   beaming   twisting   snaking

   ii slabs   pieces   chunks   blocks   iv fissures   crannies   chinks   cracks

b Write four sentences that create a sense of danger using the synonyms you selected above.

3.1: How do journeys create jeopardy?

Building your knowledge

The Body is an example of a '**coming-of-age**' **story**. The boys take a physical journey of about 20 miles, from their home in Castle Rock, along the railway track and through the countryside, to the place where a boy has died, near a river. However, they also go on an inner, mental journey – confronting their fears, testing their friendships and facing the reality of death for the first time.

Did you know?

Stephen King has written more than 60 novels and 200 short stories. He is best known for writing horror and **suspense**. *The Body* was made into a film called *Stand by Me* in 1986.

Activity 3

Think about the following examples of journeys. What might be the physical and mental challenges in each? An example based on *The Body* has been completed to help you.

Journey	Physical challenges	Mental challenges
Leaving hometown with friends to find a body	Long way to walk Scary dog A pond full of leeches A terrifying railway bridge	Overcoming fear and tiredness Managing friendships in difficult situations Coping with other people's fear Dealing with death for the first time
Solo sledging expedition across Antarctica		
Trip through a desert with strangers		

Key terms

coming-of-age story a story in which characters experience things that teach them about adulthood

convention a typical feature you find in a particular genre

genre a type of story, e.g. *horror, romance, adventure, science fiction*

suspense a feeling of anxious uncertainty while waiting for something to happen or become known

synonym a word or phrase that means the same, or almost the same, as another word or phrase

119

3: Journeys and discoveries

The following activities will help you to understand the writer's word choices in detail and get you ready to show your reading skills in a short **commentary**.

Activity 4

a Re-read lines 15–18 in extract 1, where the boys are looking at the dangerous bridge. For each of the **adverbs** or **adverbials** that describe how they speak, explain what you think they suggest about the character and what he is thinking and feeling. An example has been provided to help you.

'Chris said softly'

> Chris speaks softly because he is shocked when he looks at the bridge, and is perhaps a bit overwhelmed by the challenge ahead.

'Teddy said in that brisk, arrogant way'

'Vern said uneasily'

b Discuss which of the boys is most and least willing to take the risk of crossing the bridge.

c Read a student's answer below, along with the teacher's comment. Find the three quotations the student has used and the explanations they provide.

> Vern is the boy who is most unhappy about the bridge. His words are said 'uneasily', which suggests that he does not feel comfortable. In addition, he is the boy who brings up the idea that a train might be due, which shows that he is worrying about the risk. Vern also shows his doubt when he argues with Teddy, even though Teddy is described as 'arrogant' and some people might not want to argue with someone like that. Finally, the narrator describes Vern 'looking down at the fast, bland river' as if he can't take his eyes off the danger. Overall, this shows that Vern is the boy least willing to undertake the dangerous crossing.

This is a good explanation because you have used three quotations from the text. I like the way you have embedded the quotations in your own sentences. You have also explained clearly how each piece of evidence shows Vern's feelings.

d Write a short paragraph explaining which boy you think is most willing to take the risk of crossing the bridge. Use at least one **quotation** in your explanation.

3.1: How do journeys create jeopardy?

Putting it all together

Activity 5

a In *The Body*, the writer builds the jeopardy in different ways. Complete a table like the one below. For each of these ways, select quotations from the text. In the third column, explain how the evidence builds the jeopardy. An example has been provided to help you.

How jeopardy is built	Evidence from the text	Explanation
The **setting**	'steep' slope 'straggly, tough-looking bushes and slabs of grey rock' 'dirty collars of foam around some of the rocks' 'smelled like a laundry hamper'	The steep slope means that if the boys fall from the bridge, they are likely to plummet into the river. The 'straggly' bushes and 'slabs of grey rock' could hurt them, and the river is dirty and smelly, which creates even more danger.
The characters		
The crossing		

b Using the table you have completed and your answers in activity 4 to help you, write an answer to the question below.

> How does Stephen King build a feeling of jeopardy in *The Body*?

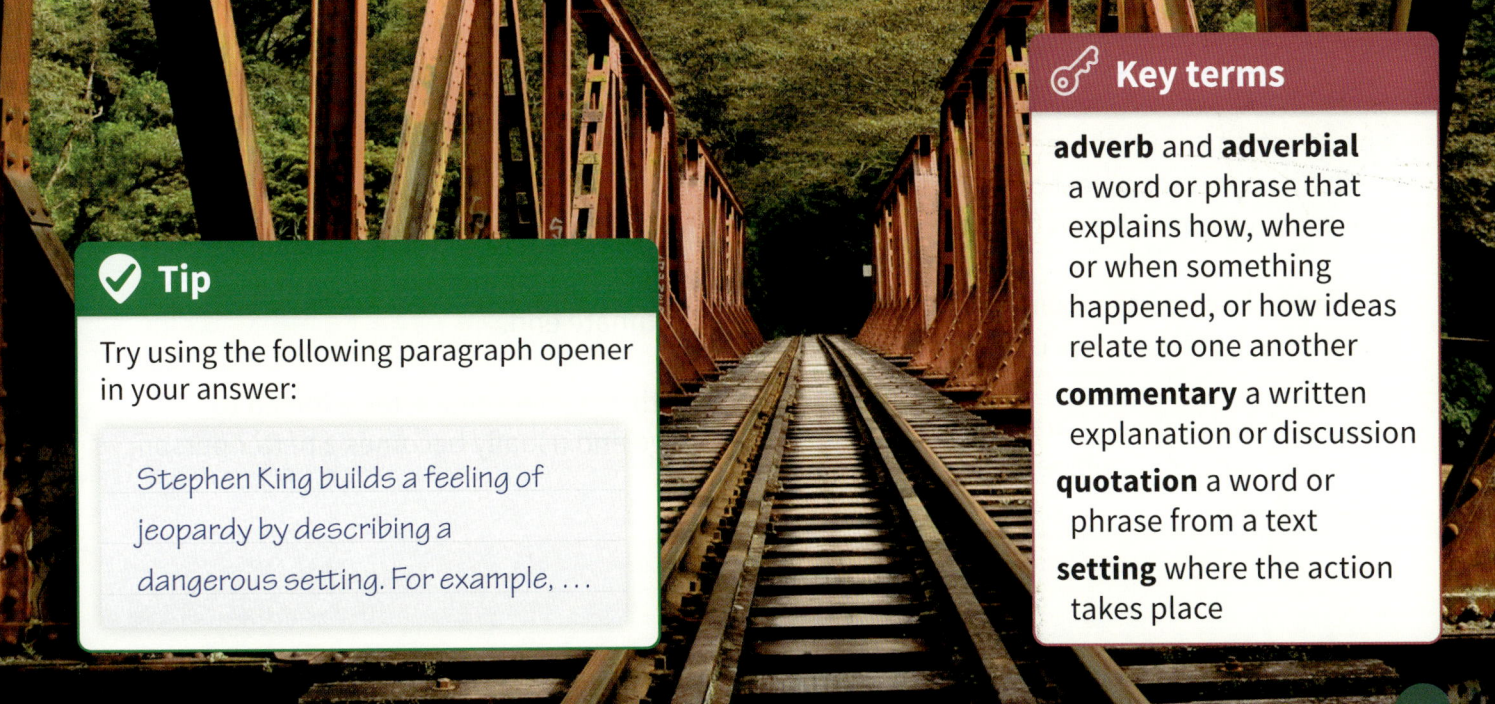

Tip

Try using the following paragraph opener in your answer:

> Stephen King builds a feeling of jeopardy by describing a dangerous setting. For example, …

Key terms

adverb and **adverbial** a word or phrase that explains how, where or when something happened, or how ideas relate to one another

commentary a written explanation or discussion

quotation a word or phrase from a text

setting where the action takes place

121

3: Journeys and discoveries

3.2 What is a quest?

In this unit, you will:
- learn to identify the main features of a quest and some other story types
- explore first-person narrative and inference
- write a scene for your own quest story, using key conventions.

What's the big idea?
In his book *The Seven Basic Plots*, Christopher Booker outlines seven story types. A journey is a key element in several of these plot types. Our focus for this unit is on quest stories. In many quest stories, in which the protagonist has to achieve a special task, the journey is also a metaphor for the character 'discovering' or developing themselves.

In this unit, you will respond to part of a quest story. According to Greek myth, Perseus had to kill the **antagonist** Medusa, who had a head of live snakes and turned anyone who looked at her to stone.

Key term
antagonist main opponent

Activity 1

Look at the seven basic plots listed below. For each plot, think of an example, drawn from your knowledge of stories in novels, plays, TV or film.

Overcoming the monster: the main character has to defeat a monster or an evil force.

The quest: the main character journeys to fetch an important object or reach a special place, facing obstacles on the way.

Comedy: characters encounter confusion or frustration but happiness is always achieved.

Rags to riches: a poor character becomes rich (or gains power or happiness), loses it all and regains it all.

Voyage and return: the main character goes to a new strange land, overcomes obstacles and returns with new knowledge.

Tragedy: the main character has a tragic flaw or makes a great mistake and comes to an unfortunate end.

Rebirth: the main character is forced to change and usually becomes a better person.

3.2: What is a quest?

The extract below is from a modern retelling of Perseus' quest, from Medusa's point of view. Here she watches from the cliff top as Perseus unpacks his boat.

Extract from *Medusa* by Jessie Burton

He didn't hurl the sandals he'd been trying on, but placed them down with **deference**, as if they were made of glass and might shatter. I saw how the sandals had wings: beautiful white feathers with pale pink tips. [...]

Daphne in particular peered down in curiosity, for she loved anything beautiful –
5 but most of my other snakes began to **writhe**. They didn't like those sandals.

It's all right, I said to them. Look – Perseus doesn't like them either.

It was true, for Perseus was gladly pulling on a much-worn, battered pair of sandals instead. I liked them for their neat practicality, their style and **subtle** flair, just the same as their owner's. [...]

10 I liked everything about Perseus, and my liking felt endless.

He pulled out the sword from underneath the **goatskin**, and finally I saw it in its full glory. It was enormous. It turned the deck gold in the sunlight – and it was far too heavy for him. The blade was straight and true, so sharp it could only have been **hammered** by a god. Perseus could barely lift it. There was a ruby at the
15 centre of the **hilt**, and from where I watched, it twinkled like a gleaming ball of blood.

I felt uneasy, looking at that sword. [...] Perseus was **ungainly** with it; an unprepared but enthusiastic warrior. He laid it down, then pulled out a helmet, which he held as if it might explode in his hands.
20 After placing the helmet on the deck, he reached again under the goatskin and dragged out a shining shield.

I was **mesmerised** by this shield – as too, of course, was Daphne. This was even better than the sandals. She wanted it, I wanted it – all of us hiding behind the rock wanted it. The shield
25 was smooth and round, as if the moon had fallen from the sky.

---

deference – behaviour that shows respect
Daphne – one of the snakes on Medusa's head
writhe – twist and turn
subtle – not obvious
goatskin – covering over the boat

hammered – shaped by beating
hilt – sword handle
ungainly – clumsy
mesmerised – amazed, fascinated

3: Journeys and discoveries

⭐ Boosting your vocabulary

Writers choose their words carefully. The activity below focuses on some key vocabulary in the source text, which has been highlighted on page 123.

> ✅ **Tip**
>
> Remember to check the meanings of any words you are unsure of in a dictionary.

Activity 2

Notice how the author's word choices make each of Perseus' weapons seem special.

| 'the sandals had wings: beautiful white feathers with pale pink tips.' | 'The blade was straight and true, so sharp it could only have been hammered by a god.' |

| '…pulled out a helmet, which he held as if it might explode in his hands.' | 'The shield was smooth and round, as if the moon had fallen from the sky.' |

a Create a new description for each object, one that highlights its beauty or emphasises its danger. Use the words below to help you.

armoured   circular   delicate   engraved
gleaming   golden   luminous   mirrored
pointed   polished   powerful   razor-edged
robust   sturdy   velvety   weighty

b Re-read the description of the sword's hilt:

> 'There was a ruby at the centre of the hilt, and from where I watched, it twinkled like a gleaming ball of blood.'

  i Why do you think the sword is decorated with a ruby?
  ii What does the word 'gleaming' suggest about the jewel?
  iii What is effective about the **simile** that the writer has chosen here?

124

3.2: What is a quest?

Building your knowledge

This is an unusual retelling of part of Perseus' quest, because it's his **nemesis** Medusa who is telling us what's going on, with the writer using a **first-person narrative**. Medusa has become the hero of her own story! Although she doesn't get to go on an actual quest journey, she does experience self-discovery, when a character discovers new things about themselves. This is an example of an inner, mental journey.

First-person stories can be powerful because they give us insight into one character's thoughts and feelings. On the other hand, we might feel more distant from other characters. In this case, we only know what Perseus is *doing*, not what he is thinking or feeling, so we need to **infer** his thoughts and feelings.

Activity 3

How do you think Perseus might be feeling, based on his actions? What meaning can you infer from what Medusa says? Complete a table like the one below.

Medusa says…	Perseus might be thinking / feeling…
'He didn't hurl the sandals he'd been trying on, but placed them down with deference, as if they were made of glass and might shatter.'	Sandals with feathers! Will they help me to fly like a bird? They must be precious. Maybe I'll be able to escape from Medusa by lifting off into the sky.
'… Perseus was gladly pulling on a much-worn, battered pair of sandals instead.'	
'The blade was straight and true, so sharp it could only have been hammered by a god. Perseus could barely lift it.'	
'He … pulled out a helmet, which he held as if it might explode in his hands.'	
'he reached again under the goatskin and dragged out a shining shield.'	

Key terms

first-person narrative a story told by someone as if they were involved in the events themselves, using first-person pronouns, e.g. *I* and *we*

infer to work something out from what is seen, said or done, even though it is not stated directly

nemesis an enemy or competitor that cannot be avoided

simile a comparison of one thing to another, using *as* or *like*, e.g. *He swam like a fish*

Did you know?

It can be harder to find examples of questers who are women in myths and legends because traditionally men were seen as the characters of courage and direct action. Nowadays, female and non-binary questers are more common in novels, films, computer games and TV programmes. For example, Merida, the protagonist of the film *Brave*, goes on a quest and journey of self-discovery.

125

3: Journeys and discoveries

In activity 3, you identified how an author *shows* internal feelings by exploring what Perseus's actions reveal about what he is thinking and feeling. Now you are going to write your own first-person narrative, taking on the character of a quester and describing your weapons and your thoughts and feelings about the task you must achieve.

Activity 4

Before creating your own story quest, practise your skills by writing an **internal monologue** as Perseus as he considers his weapons. Remember that a monologue is a speech by one character and an internal monologue is speech in a character's head.

Imagine you are Perseus talking to yourself or writing a diary.

- As you take each weapon from its place, describe it.
- Add thoughts and feelings about the task ahead.

Here is an example of how one student chose to begin this task and then commented on their approach:

> I have reached my destination and I have an enormous task ahead. Without further ado, I must slay Medusa, the snake-headed monster who turns everyone she looks upon to stone. Naturally, I am afeared. Alack, I know not if I am strong or brave enough.
>
> Behold these sandals with feathers! Delicate and luminous they are, with pink tips! Will they help me to fly like a bird? Maybe I shall escape from the snake-headed woman by lifting off into the sky.

- First-person narrative to recount the quester's actions
- **Archaic** words and sentence structures to help create the feel of a myth
- Insights into emotions of the storyteller
- Vocabulary to make the narrative more precise and descriptive

✓ Tip

Archaic vocabulary and sentence structures can be used to give your writing an old-fashioned quality, suitable for a myth.
- Try word choices such as 'afeared' instead of 'frightened', 'slay' instead of 'kill'.
- Try sentence structures such as 'I know not' instead of 'I don't know'.

🔑 Key terms

archaic old-fashioned, from a different historical time

internal monologue inner speech (in someone's head)

tone the writer's feeling or attitude expressed towards their subject; in fiction it can also reflect a character's feelings and personality

126

3.2: What is a quest?

Putting it all together

Activity 5

a Plan the story elements you want to include in your own first-person quest narrative. Decide on one quester, one quest setting, one difficult task and two or three weapons.

You can choose some of the options from the groups below or use your own ideas.

The quester
A teenager who has just discovered their magical powers
A young person who needs to earn their freedom
A warrior trying to get home

Where will the quest take you?
A lonely island
A magical city
An underground labyrinth

The task ahead
Fetch a golden goblet
Rescue a child
Take back your home

Weapons
A harp that sends enemies to sleep
A venom-tipped spear
A belt that bestows great strength

b Present your ideas to a partner or small group.

Activity 6

Write the scene in which your hero (quester) unpacks their weapons. As they take each weapon from its place – which could be a special bag or hiding place – describe it and add thoughts and feelings about the task ahead.

As you write, keep the key features in mind. Stop every few lines and read over your work to check that you are including:

- first-person narrative to recount the storyteller's actions
- insights into the storyteller's emotions
- vocabulary to make the narrative more precise and descriptive
- archaic words and sentence structures to help create the **tone** and feel of a myth.

Stretch yourself

Try writing from the point of view of another character observing the quester, as in the extract. Remember that you won't be able to reveal the quester's thoughts and feelings directly, only your own.

3: Journeys and discoveries

3.3 Why start with a journey?

In this unit, you will:
- learn to recognise key plot conventions
- identify word choices and literary devices and comment on their effects
- analyse the presentation of a journey, using close textual reference.

What's the big idea?
Journeys can be a source of jeopardy – plunging characters into danger – and they are also the basis of quest stories, in which characters travel physically and metaphorically, to find special objects and achieve amazing feats. A journey also makes a great inciting incident – throwing characters into new circumstances at the beginning of a story and getting the plot started.

In this unit, you will read part of *Jamaica Inn*, which was published in 1936 but set in 1816. The author called it 'a story of adventure', and it begins with its **protagonist**, Mary Yellan, on a journey to a new life.

Activity 1

An **inciting incident** is the moment that sets a character off in a new direction.

a Think of examples of inciting incidents from films, TV programmes and novels you know. For example, in *The Hobbit*, Bilbo Baggins must leave the Shire to find a precious object.

b How do you think an inciting incident impacts the reader?

Key terms

inciting incident the event that sets up the action for the rest of the story

protagonist main character

The next extract is from the opening of *Jamaica Inn* where a coach and horses, with Mary as a passenger, is travelling through Cornwall.

3.3: Why start with a journey?

Extract from *Jamaica Inn* by Daphne du Maurier

It was a cold grey day in late November. The weather had changed overnight, when a **backing wind** brought a **granite** sky and a mizzling rain with it, and although it was now only a little after two o'clock in the afternoon the **pallor** of a winter evening seemed to have closed upon the hills, cloaking them in mist. It would be dark by four. The air was clammy cold, and for all the tightly
5   closed windows it **penetrated** the interior of the coach. The leather seats felt damp to the hands, and there must have been a small crack in the roof, because now and again little drips of rain fell softly through, smudging the leather and leaving a dark-blue stain like a splodge of ink. The wind came in gusts, at times shaking the coach as it travelled round the bend of the road, and in the exposed places on the high ground it blew with such force that the whole body of the coach trembled and
10 swayed, rocking between the high wheels like a drunken man. [...]

Mary Yellan sat in the corner, where the trickle of rain oozed through the crack in the roof. Sometimes a cold drip of moisture fell upon her shoulder, which she brushed away with impatient fingers.

She sat with her chin cupped in her hands, her eyes fixed on the window splashed with mud and
15 rain, hoping with a sort of desperate interest that some ray of light would break the heavy blanket of sky, and but a momentary trace of that lost blue heaven that had **mantled** Helford yesterday shine for an instant as **a forerunner of fortune**.

Already, though barely forty miles by road from what had been her home for three and twenty years, the hope within her heart had tired, and that rather **gallant** courage which was so large a
20 part of her, and had stood her in such stead during the long agony of her mother's illness and death, was now shaken by this first fall of rain and the nagging wind.

The country was alien to her, which was defeat in itself. As she peered through the misty window of the coach she looked out upon a different world from the one she had known only a day's journey back. How remote now and hidden perhaps for ever were the shining waters of Helford, the green
25 hills and the sloping valleys, the white cluster of cottages at the water's edge. It was a gentle rain that fell at Helford, a rain that pattered in the many trees and lost itself in the lush grass, formed into brooks and **rivulets** that emptied into the broad river, sank into the grateful soil which gave back flowers in payment.

This was a lashing, pitiless rain that stung the windows of the coach, and it soaked into a hard and
30 **barren** soil.

---

backing wind – wind that is shifting direction
granite – hard grey stone
pallor – pale, unhealthy colour
penetrated – went through or into
mantled – covered

a forerunner of fortune – sign of good luck
gallant – brave, heroic
rivulets – small streams
barren – not good enough for plants to grow

3: Journeys and discoveries

⭐ Boosting your vocabulary

Writers choose their words carefully. The activity below focuses on some key vocabulary in the source text, which has been highlighted on page 129.

Activity 2

a   Words can have different meanings depending on their **context**. Select the sentence that best shows the meaning used in the text:

   i   alien
   - An alien is sitting in the coach with Mary.
   - The countryside around is completely unfamiliar.
   - The countryside around is full of aliens.

   ii   impatient
   - Mary is annoyed by the rain dripping on her.
   - Mary is irritated by her hair.
   - Mary has been waiting for a long time for the coach.

   iii   stung
   - There are stinging insects hovering around the coach.
   - The rain is hitting Mary hard.
   - The rain is hitting the coach hard.

b   The rain is a key feature in this extract. Rank these words and phrases that refer to the damp weather in order of how bad they make it sound.

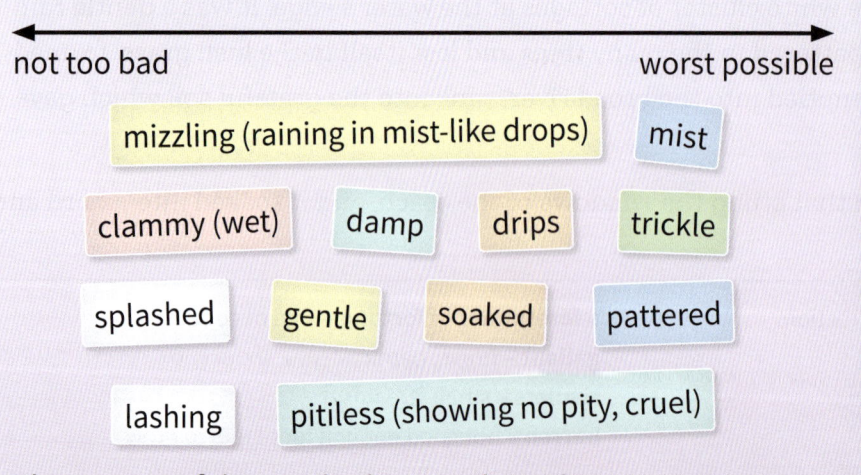

⟵──────────────────────────────⟶
not too bad   worst possible

- mizzling (raining in mist-like drops)
- mist
- clammy (wet)
- damp
- drips
- trickle
- splashed
- gentle
- soaked
- pattered
- lashing
- pitiless (showing no pity, cruel)

c   Choose two of the words above and use them in your own description of rain.

🔑 Key term

context the words that come before and after a particular word or phrase and help to clarify its meaning

3.3: Why start with a journey?

Building your knowledge

An inciting incident, sometimes known as the 'call to adventure', is the moment that sets a character off in a new direction. In Mary Yellan's case, the death of her mother means she has to move. Within a few pages, she arrives at Jamaica Inn – a dark, cold, isolated place where her ghost-like aunt and wicked uncle live. Mary becomes a servant in their house of locked rooms and creaking noises, while violent men come and go.

Did you know?

Jamaica Inn is a real place – a hotel – and according to its website, Daphne du Maurier stayed there in 1930, went out on horseback and got lost in the dark and the mist.

Activity 3

Complete a table like the one below.

a   Read the information from the novel about Mary's old life. How has each aspect of her life changed in the extract on p129?

b   Identify quotations or evidence from the extract that support your answers.

Mary Yellan's old life	Mary Yellan's new life	Supporting evidence
She lived with her mother.	Her mother has recently died, so she is now an orphan.	'her mother's illness and death'
It was sunny when she first set out on her journey.		
She lived all her life in one place.		
The rain was gentle in her old town.		
Her old town was pretty and pleasant.		
She is usually a brave and hopeful person.		

The writer focuses the reader's attention on the weather during Mary's journey (see activity 2). She uses a technique called **pathetic fallacy**, in which the weather in a scene reflects the feelings and the situation of the characters.

One example is when the writer says 'the weather had changed overnight'. The sudden change of weather reminds us of the sudden change in Mary's circumstances.

Key term

pathetic fallacy giving emotions to something non-human in the natural world to reflect a character's feelings or situation

Activity 4

a   Find two more examples of pathetic fallacy in the text.

b   What does each example of pathetic fallacy suggest about Mary and her situation?

3: Journeys and discoveries

You are going to write about the opening of *Jamaica Inn*, focusing on how the author uses details to show that Mary Yellan's life is about to change for the worse.

Key terms

cohesive device a word or phrase that links ideas together, e.g. *at the beginning, however, although*

foreshadowing a technique that gives a hint of something that will develop later

Activity 5

There are clues in the opening of *Jamaica Inn* that hint at a more difficult life ahead for Mary. This is called **foreshadowing**. For each element of the story below, a-d, consider what it suggests about what might happen to Mary. The first one has been done for you.

a Uncomfortable journey such as the leaking coach

> Mary's new life might be very uncomfortable and difficult.

b Unpleasant weather such as the rain and wind

c Changes in Mary such as her mother's death

d Changes in the surroundings such as the bleak countryside

When you write about a text and the author's intentions, you must:
- use formal language
- organise your ideas into paragraphs
- use short quotations to back up your ideas
- connect your ideas using **cohesive devices**.

Activity 6

Read the following question.

> How does the opening of *Jamaica Inn* show us that Mary Yellan's life is about to change for the worse?

a Read the first draft of one student's opening paragraph in response to this question, opposite. Note the teacher's comments.

b Explain how the student has followed this advice in their second draft and improved their paragraph. Identify two cohesive devices the student has used in their answer.

c List three other examples of cohesive devices you can think of.

132

3.3: Why start with a journey?

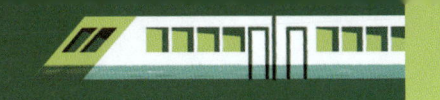

First draft:

Mary Yellan is on a journey. The coach she is in is really old and a bit nasty inside. It's not comfy at all. It's like it's about to fall over when it says it is swaying.

> Try using cohesive devices to introduce some of your sentences and link your ideas together. Also, choose more formal vocabulary. This will make your writing more precise and make you sound more knowledgeable. You need to say what effect the author's choices have. For example, putting the character in an uncomfortable old coach is a hint that Mary's new life might be equally difficult.

Second draft:

At the beginning of the novel, Mary Yellan is on a journey. The coach she is travelling in is old, cold and damp, which makes the journey seem uncomfortable. The coach seems about to fall over because it is swaying 'like a drunken man'. From the very start, Mary is put in a difficult situation, which makes the reader think her new life might be difficult.

Stretch yourself

Choose the opening of another novel that starts with a journey and consider the clues the writer gives about the new life the character seems to be heading towards. Write your ideas in bullet points. Books you could choose include *Dracula* by Bram Stoker, *Alice's Adventures in Wonderland* by Lewis Carroll or *The Arrival* by Shaun Tan.

Putting it all together

Activity 7

a Using your answers from activities 4–6 to help, write your own answer to the question:

> How does the opening of *Jamaica Inn* show us that Mary Yellan's life is about to change for the worse?

Remember to:
- use formal language
- organise your ideas into paragraphs
- use short quotations to back up your ideas
- connect your ideas using cohesive devices.

b After completing a first draft, self-assess your work against this list using a highlighter to show at least one place where you have done each.

3: Journeys and discoveries

3.4 How can poetry explore journeys?

In this unit, you will:
- learn how texts are influenced by the contexts in which they are written
- rehearse and perform a poetry reading
- recognise poetic features and comment on their effect.

What's the big idea?

So far, you have studied journeys in fiction. In real life too, journeys are revealing and compelling. They make us ask questions. What makes people want to travel? How do people cope when they are forced to travel? What kind of hardships or dangers do they endure? What happens when they reach their destination?

In this unit, you are going to look at a poem about refugees – people forced to leave their country to seek refuge (safety).

Activity 1

Before you read the poem, think about its context. Make a mind map or spider diagram to include the following:
- emotions that people forced to leave their homes and seek refuge might experience
- things that refugees might want to carry with them and things they may have to leave behind
- challenges that refugees have to cope with.

The poet Wang Ping grew up in China, but she left in her late twenties and moved to the United States of America. In the poem opposite, she writes about the experiences of refugees.

'Things We Carry on the Sea' by Wang Ping

We carry tears in our eyes: good-bye father, good-bye mother

We carry soil in small bags: may home never fade in our hearts

We carry names, stories, memories of our villages, fields, boats

We carry scars from **proxy** wars of greed

5 We carry **carnage** of mining, droughts, floods, **genocides**

We carry dust of our families and neighbors **incinerated** in **mushroom clouds**

We carry our islands sinking under the sea

We carry our hands, feet, bones, hearts and best minds for a new life

We carry **diplomas**: medicine, engineer, nurse, education, math, poetry, even if they mean nothing to the other shore

10 We carry railroads, plantations, laundromats, bodegas, taco trucks, farms, factories, nursing homes, hospitals, schools, temples… built on our ancestors' backs

We carry old homes along the spine, new dreams in our chests

We carry yesterday, today and tomorrow

We're orphans of the wars forced upon us

We're refugees of the sea rising from industrial wastes

15 And we carry our **mother tongues**

爱 (ai), حب (hubb), ליבע (libe), amor, love

平安 (ping'an), سلام (salaam), shalom, paz, peace

希望 (xi'wang), أمل ('amal), hofenung, esperanza, hope, hope, hope

As we drift… in our rubber boats… from shore… to shore… to shore…

---

proxy – something used to represent something else
carnage – violent killing
genocides – murders of large numbers of people
incinerated – destroyed by burning
mushroom clouds – clouds associated with bombs and explosions
diplomas – certificates of education
mother tongues – first languages

3: Journeys and discoveries

Activity 2

a   According to the poem, what sorts of events and experiences drive people from their homes?

b   Check all the things that the poem says people carry. Which ones can actually be physically carried? Which cannot?

c   How many lists can you find in this poem? Why do you think the poet has used lists?

d   What languages do you recognise in the poem? Why do you think the poet chose to include words from a range of languages?

e   How is **ellipsis** (…) used in the poem?

Key terms

audience the people or person for whom a text is written or performed

ellipsis three dots (…) used to show a pause or to indicate that a word or words have been left out

recital a performance

Activity 3

Prepare a **recital** of this poem.

a   Read it through multiple times to ensure you are familiar with the language and content.

b   Annotate the poem to show how you will read different parts. For example, where will you pause, and how long for? Where will you use a louder, quieter, deeper or lighter voice to convey the emotions in the poem?

c   Check pronunciation with a speaker of the languages used in the poem or using a web-based translating tool. Make notes on how the words are pronounced.

d   Perform the poem to your chosen **audience** and evaluate your performance.
   - Did you read fluently, without hesitation?
   - Did you adapt your reading voice to match the emotions of the poem?
   - What did you find easier and more difficult about this task?
   - How could you improve your poetry recital next time?

3.4: How can poetry explore journeys?

⭐ Boosting your vocabulary

Writers choose their words carefully. The activity below focuses on some key vocabulary in the source text, which has been highlighted on page 135.

Activity 4

Many American English words are now commonly used by English speakers all over the world because of the influence of American films and TV programmes and as English becomes more and more a global language. However, in the poem you may have noticed some unfamiliar words:

- 'math' – English speakers in the UK would usually say 'maths'
- 'laundromats' – in the UK, these are 'laundrettes'
- 'bodegas' – small shops in Spanish-speaking areas that UK English speakers might call corner shops or local stores

a Circle the American English words in the sentences below and link them to the British English equivalent. The first one has been done for you.

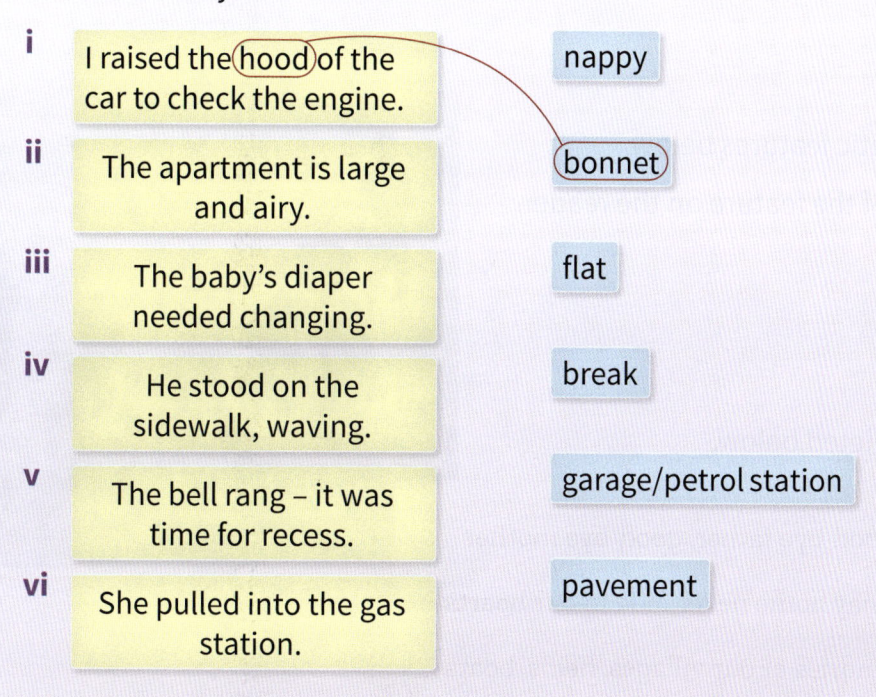

i   I raised the (hood) of the car to check the engine. — nappy

ii The apartment is large and airy. — (bonnet)

iii The baby's diaper needed changing. — flat

iv He stood on the sidewalk, waving. — break

v   The bell rang – it was time for recess. — garage/petrol station

vi She pulled into the gas station. — pavement

b Write three sentences of your own that use American English vocabulary. Check that a partner can identify the words you have used.

❓ Did you know?

Around the world, there are about 1.5 billion people who speak English. Many of them have learned it as an additional language to their first language. There are many varieties of English, such as American English, Ugandan English and Indian English.

⬆ Stretch yourself

How do you think it might feel to hear these American English words every day or be expected to use them instead of British English? How does this help you to understand what the poet might be feeling?

137

3: Journeys and discoveries

Building your knowledge

This poem is mainly a list of 'We carry' statements, each a single-line **stanza**. This listing technique seems simple, but the things that are carried are a range of complex ideas. The poet emphasises the **abstract** things that refugees take with them, such as sadness, memories and loss. The refugees haven't been able to take many real objects with them, so while they aren't weighed down by bags, they are still burdened.

The poem is written from the point of view of the refugees, using the **first-person plural pronoun** 'we'. The poet positions herself as one of the people in the poem, perhaps drawing on some of her own experiences or the experiences of people she knows. The poem explores things that refugees have in common as well as the differences between them.

You are going to write a series of paragraphs about this poem, exploring what the poet says and how she says it. The following activities will support you in this task.

Key terms

abstract existing as an idea but not having a physical reality

first-person plural pronoun *we* and *us* are ways of speaking in the first person about more than one person

repetition using the same word or phrase more than once

stanza a group of lines in a poem with a line space before and after it

Activity 5

Annotate the poem by:

a finding examples of the poetic features below

b commenting on the effect of the feature on the reader.
  - first-person pronouns
  - listing
  - ellipsis
  - repetition

An example has been completed below.

> We carry tears in our eyes: good-bye father, good-bye mother
>
> We carry soil in small bags: may home never fade in our hearts
>
> We carry names, stories, memories of our villages, fields, boats

Feature: **repetition**
The poem is mainly a list of single lines beginning with 'We carry'. This emphasises the number of people who are making these journeys as well as the number of things — real and abstract — they are carrying.

138

3.4: How can poetry explore journeys?

Putting it all together

Think about the context of this poem and what it is saying about the poet's experience and the experiences of refugees in general. Think also about your performance of the poem and which parts of it have a strong impact on you.

Activity 6

Using your answers from activity 5 to help you, write an answer to the following question:

> How does the poet convey the experiences of refugees in the poem?

Your answer should include:

- your thoughts and feelings about the poem and the language choices that had an effect on you
- your knowledge of the poetic features in the poem and your ideas about their effect.

Tip

When writing about a poem, do not just point out its features. Make your comments about the *effect* of the poem on the reader. Try using sentence openers like the ones below:

> This repetition has the effect of…
>
> draws attention to…
>
> The lists create…
>
> The sound of… suggests that…
>
> I think this is a powerful line because…

139

3: Journeys and discoveries

3.5 What is travel writing?

In this unit, you will:
- learn about the key conventions of travel writing
- identify the effects of grammatical features in travel writing
- write about a journey around your neighbourhood.

What's the big idea?

Travel writing has a long history. Starting with the Greek Pausanius and the Persian Nasir Khusraw, travellers have written descriptions of their travels. Some early travel writing is in diary form, written by sailors and naturalists as they sailed around the world. In this unit we'll focus on the conventions of travel writing and the effects of typical travel writing features.

Activity 1

Consider the following statements. Which do you think are true and which are false?

a Travel writing is about visiting other continents.
b Travel writers have to be rich.
c Travel writers always travel by plane.
d Travel writing is completely factual.
e Travel writing is only published in books.

In the **travel writing** opposite, Alastair Humphreys is travelling by bike. He is close to home, cycling through nearby neighbourhoods and reflecting on what he finds there.

Key term

travel writing writing produced during or after a journey, describing it in order to inform and/or entertain readers

Did you know?

Stories of enslavement often contain sections of travel writing, describing enforced journeys and individual escapes. One famous example is *Twelve Years a Slave* by Solomon Northup.

A blog post by Alastair Humphreys

I began the day amongst Victorian terraces [...] Placards saying 'Thank you NHS' and a fluttering Union Jack. [...] A row of shops, as noted often before across my map: kebab house, Chinese, Indian, a garage door shop (that's a first), bookmaker, and a fried chicken joint. It is a traditional, tired one street town of independent though struggling shops, pubs, kebab joints and a big new Domino's pizza place. [...]

All this was more or less what I expected from looking at my map before cycling here. What I had not anticipated was that behind all this was a new area of **clapboard** houses and commuter apartments. [...] Clapboard buildings painted pastel shades, drainage **culverts** landscaped into trickling streams, wooden balconies and pots of geraniums. [...] They hardly matched the traditional building conventions of the region. I wondered whether this new town will merge with the old, whether its vibe will overtake the traditional terraces down the road, if cappuccino to go will trump a cup of tea in the cafe. [...]

I carried on my way, heading through a low underpass beneath the railway into an area of riverside reed beds and streams, home to reed buntings and reed and sedge warblers. Damselflies flitted in the sunshine. Pink and white **marsh mallows** grew along the verge.

I sampled a few blackberries – they are getting sweeter, but not quite ready yet. The hawthorn berries are also ripening quickly now. The footpath ran along the route of an old railway line and hunks of concrete from the old demolished factories were dotted around. A **bird hide** had been erected, a simple wooden wall of planks with two horizontal gaps sliced through it, one at adult eye height and one for children. I saw nothing more exciting than a few pigeons, despite a sign suggesting I may spy kingfishers, teal, egrets, water rail and gadwalls here at various times.

I liked it out here on the marsh tucked into a tight curve of the river, the sky big blue and empty, the paper factory's five chimneys smoking away in the distance, and only the sound of the breeze rustling the reeds. The river is the boundary of my map, more or less. The other side, unknown ground, looks so tempting to me as always.

---

clapboard – painted wood panels
culverts – tunnels that carry water under roads
marsh mallows – plants that grow in marshy areas
bird hide – wooden hut to watch birds from

3: Journeys and discoveries

⭐ Boosting your vocabulary

Writers choose their words carefully. The activity below focuses on some key vocabulary in the source text, which has been highlighted on page 141.

Activity 2

a   Re-read the descriptions below and identify the correct meaning from the list.

   i   'It is a traditional, tired one street town…'

   The town:
   - is busy with many streets
   - has layers of streets full of weary people
   - is very small, familiar and run-down.

   ii   'Clapboard buildings painted pastel shades, drainage culverts landscaped into trickling streams, wooden balconies and pots of geraniums.'

   The houses:
   - are surrounded by manufactured drainage systems
   - are painted in bright colours
   - have flowers on their iron balconies.

   iii   'The footpath ran along the route of an old railway line and hunks of concrete from the old demolished factories were dotted around.'

   The writer:
   - cycled a path that went past factories
   - ran along the railway track
   - noticed the old railway line was covered in hunks of concrete.

b   Choose one word that you have learned from reading this text (it may be in the glossary) and write two different sentences to show your understanding of it.

3.5: What is travel writing?

Building your knowledge

Travel writing is usually a first-person narrative. It is factual (**non-fiction**), but it also includes the writer's opinions and reflections. Rather than just being a list of places visited, the writer tries to entertain the reader by being funny or dramatic, descriptive or thoughtful. Some travel writing tells us as much about the writer as the place they visited, so can be considered **autobiographical**.

Imagine how short Alastair Humphreys' blog would be if he just wrote about where he cycled: 'I went past some shops, through a residential area, under the railway, and along a railway line to the river and the marsh.' Instead, at each stage of the journey the writer notices tiny details.

Activity 3

In the extract you have just read, find:
- a clue to when the journey took place
- a list of birds
- an example of **contrast**
- a fact
- an opinion
- three different stages of the journey.

The writer uses a range of grammatical features to add detailed description to his journey, which helps to make the text more interesting and engaging.

The writer uses **minor sentences** like 'Placards saying "Thank you NHS" and a fluttering Union Jack' to create a sense of passing by on his cycling journey.

Adjectives and **adjectival phrases** help to inform the reader and allow them to picture what the writer can see, for example 'big blue and empty'.

Prepositional phrases such as 'through a low underpass' explain where things are in relation to each other on the journey and also function as cohesive devices.

Key terms

adjective and **adjectival phrase** a word or phrase that describes a person or thing

autobiographical based on the writer's life

contrast difference between two or more things; also, to compare to show a difference

minor sentence sometimes known as a sentence fragment, a sentence without a main verb or subject

non-fiction real events or factual information

prepositional phrase a phrase that begins with a preposition (e.g. *between*, *near*, *by*, *beyond*) and tells the reader about location and place

143

3: Journeys and discoveries

Activity 4

Complete a table like the one below. This will help you prepare for creating a piece of travel writing in activity 6.

a   Find at least one more example from the text to match each feature identified below.

b   Complete the final column of the table to show how you'll use each technique in your writing.

Name of feature	Example(s) from text	Example(s) from text	How will I use this in my writing?
First person	'The river is the boundary of my map'		
Prepositional phrases	'in the distance'		
Descriptive **noun phrases**	'the sound of the breeze rustling the reeds' / 'hunks of concrete from the old demolished factories'		
Interesting **verb** choices	'Damselflies *flitted*.' / 'the marsh *tucked* into a tight curve'		
Adjectives and adjectival phrases	'getting sweeter, but not quite ready yet'		

🔑 Key terms

noun phrase a noun plus information before and/or after the noun

verb a word or group of words that express an action, event or state, e.g. the boy *eats*, tigers *prowl*, the building *exists*

3.5: What is travel writing?

Putting it all together

Activity 5

Your task to create a piece of non-fiction travel writing has five planning steps:

Step 1: Imagine taking a short journey around your local neighbourhood. You could make your way through streets, parks and shopping centres, along rivers and canals, over bridges, between office blocks and under subways.

Step 2: Make plenty of notes and try to capture what you imagine and what it makes you think about.

Step 3: Decide where your travel writing is going to begin and end.

Step 4: Choose four or five paragraph headings – one for each part of your journey. The paragraph headings for Alastair Humphreys' cycle journey might start like this:
- Starting the journey – the old part of town
- The new parts of town and what I think about them
- The riverside…

Step 5: For each paragraph in your plan, add:
- something to describe – try to use a noun phrase
- an opinion – try to use adjectives or an adjectival phrase
- a thought or reflection – try starting with 'I wonder…' or 'It makes me think…'

For example, this student took a cycle ride through their town, which started on a busy shopping street. For their second paragraph, they have chosen a quiet residential road:

> Something to describe – the trees planted at intervals along the grass verges
>
> An opinion – the trees make the road lighter and brighter
>
> A thought – this must give the people something to tell the seasons by

Activity 6

a Write a first draft of your travel writing, using your paragraph plan. Try to include as many of the features listed in the activity 4 table as you can.

b Review your writing: read it aloud or share it with a partner. Check that you have included at least three of the features listed in activity 3.

3: Journeys and discoveries

3.6 Why travel sustainably?

In this unit, you will:
- learn about features of persuasive texts
- explore the effects of persuasive techniques on the reader
- write and present a speech confidently in front of an audience.

What's the big idea?

It's possible to get to most countries of the world by aeroplane, car, boat or train. However, tourists are becoming more aware of the carbon footprint of their travels (the amount of greenhouse gases created), as well as considering other environmental impacts of their journeys, such as waste and pollution. Our focus in this unit is persuasive techniques that encourage people to travel sustainably.

In this unit, you will read **persuasive** texts about sustainable tourism, which means travelling for leisure in a way that reduces the impact on the environment. You will then write a speech persuading people to go on a sustainable holiday.

Key term

persuasive making you want to do or believe something

Did you know?

Holidaymakers cause a 40% surge in marine litter (rubbish found in the sea) entering the Mediterranean Sea each summer, 95% of it plastic. (WWF, 2018)

Activity 1

a What do you know about sustainability?

b What do you think a sustainable holiday might involve?

c Do you think it's important to travel sustainably?

d How might you persuade someone to have a sustainable holiday? Which of the techniques below would you use?

alliteration   inclusive pronouns   colloquial language

pun   evidence and statistics   emotive language

imperative verbs   positive noun phrases   direct address

technical information   repetition   rhetorical questions

modal verbs   hyperbole

146

3.6: Why travel sustainably?

Read the following extracts from an article about sustainable holidays, published in 2019.

'Electric road trip through Switzerland'

You may be trying not to burn fuel, but that doesn't mean **forgoing** the delicious unrolling of a road trip. Switzerland has launched a route for electric vehicles, with 300 charging stations covering 1,970km through some of Europe's most eye-popping scenery, in a country committed to maintaining 30% woodland coverage. The 'grand electric road trip' route goes over five **Alpine passes**, by 22 lakes, the vineyards of the Montreux Riviera, through foodie Ticino, or the Jura. It launched quietly two years ago but is being given a big push for 2020 by the **Swiss tourist board**, as sustainable travel is the focus.

forgoing – giving up, going without
Alpine passes – routes through the Alps mountain region
Swiss tourist board – official organisation that encourages travellers to visit Switzerland

'Easy train to Sweden'

A new collection of European rail holidays [has been designed] by Original Travel. [...] The journey to Gothenburg starts with a night out in Hamburg before a ferry from Germany to Denmark, then it's on to Gothenburg by train to devour some cinnamon buns. Two nights on the island of Marstrand, home to **ornate** wooden houses, **precedes** one in a floating hotel on one of many tiny islands visited by ferry. Then it's back the same way, with a **last hurrah** in Hamburg.

ornate – decorated with complicated designs
precedes – comes before
last hurrah – final event, usually joyful

'Wildlife safari, Spain'

Griffon vultures, bustards, Spanish imperial eagles, great spotted cuckoos and larks are among the species to tick off on a wildlife adventure to Extremadura, in western Spain. This is one of Naturetrek's new no-fly group trips, which also aim to minimise disposable plastic use. After the ferry to Santander from Plymouth, there's a boat ride in the Bay of Biscay to spot whales and dolphins, before a rail journey to spend two nights in Madrid for some **urban** bird-watching in the **Real Jardín Botanico**.

urban – relating to a town or city
Real Jardin Botanico – Royal Botanic Garden (a garden where plants are labelled)

3: Journeys and discoveries

Activity 2

Use **scanning** skills to decide whether the statements below are true or false. Scanning involves searching a text for the information you need, but not reading every single word. You can do this by quickly looking for key words, such as the place names below.

a Switzerland is a good destination for people with electric cars.
b In Switzerland, you can buy delicious cakes called 'unrollings'.
c The route for electric cars passes mountains, vineyards and lakes.
d From Gothenburg, you travel through Hamburg to Marstrand.
e On Marstrand, you can see vultures on safari.
f There is a botanical garden in Madrid.

⭐ Boosting your vocabulary

Writers choose their words carefully. The activity below focuses on some key vocabulary in the source text, which has been highlighted on page 147.

Activity 3

a i   Think of a a synonym for 'devour'.
   ii Why do you think the writer has chosen the word 'devour' and not its synonym?
   iii Use the word 'devour' in your own sentence.

b The word 'sustainable' means 'able to be held at a certain rate'. Because of the climate crisis, sustainability has become an important concept. Come up with a definition for:

   sustainable fashion   sustainable travel

   sustainable development

🔑 Key terms

alliteration using the same letter or sound at the beginning of several words for special effect

colloquial language informal words or phrases that are suitable for ordinary conversation, rather than formal speech or writing

direct address addressing the reader as *you*

emotive language word choices that create a strong emotional reaction in the reader

evidence and statistics data and facts

scanning reading quickly to find something specific

technical information specialised words or phrases

3.6: Why travel sustainably?

> 💡 **Building your knowledge**

People who sell holidays have to be persuasive. They will use facts and descriptions that emphasise the attractions of a destination and leave out negative information. They will appeal to readers' senses, explaining how the trip will relax and excite them. They will make the journey sound thrilling and worthwhile. To sell a sustainable holiday, the travel company also needs to appeal to the reader's desire to be eco-friendly.

The writer uses a range of persuasive techniques in the extracts on p147 to persuade the reader to travel sustainably and to book a holiday with them.

- They use **colloquial language** to create a friendly atmosphere and a conversational relationship with the reader, e.g. 'Then it's back the same way'.
- The writer also addresses the reader as 'you'. This technique is called **direct address** and has the effect of building a personal relationship with the reader.
- **Emotive language** is often used in persuasive writing because it appeals to the readers' emotions, e.g. 'the delicious unrolling of a road trip'.

Activity 4

Complete a table like the one below. Find an example of each of the persuasive techniques in the extracts from the article about sustainable holidays.

Technique	Example from text	Definition
Alliteration	'a boat ride in the Bay of Biscay'	Repetition of words starting with the same sound
Emotive language		Word choices that appeal to readers' emotions
Colloquial language		Everyday language
Evidence and statistics		Data and facts used to support an argument
Direct address		Addressing the reader as 'you'
Positive noun phrases		Positive or informative adjectives to modify nouns
Technical information		Specialised words or phrases

149

3: Journeys and discoveries

Activity 5

a   Using the extracts on p147 and your own ideas, do some research about sustainable travel. You'll use your ideas in activity 6 to write a speech.

b   Create an itinerary (a plan of events relating to a journey) for a sustainable holiday. Think about:
   - the modes of travel
   - where travellers will stay
   - what activities you will offer.

c   Think of some example sentences that you might end up using in your speech, using the persuasive techniques you have been studying.

⬆ Stretch yourself

'Sustainable travel means missing out on amazing experiences.' Do you agree or disagree with this statement? How would you persuade someone of your opinion? Use the extracts on p147 and the persuasive techniques on p149 to help you.

3.6: Why travel sustainably?

🧩 Putting it all together

Activity 6

You're going to give a speech about the holiday itinerary you created in activity 5. To give an effective speech, you need to be well prepared.

a Plan the most persuasive ways to talk about the holiday. Aim to include many of the persuasive techniques you have been learning about.

✏ b Write your speech.

c Next, reduce your speech to notes. You will need to look up at your audience while you are speaking, so avoid having every word written down. Instead, write down key words and phrases that will help you to remember the rest.

d Practise your speech, ideally in front of a partner, someone at home or a mirror. Aim to make your delivery fluent and confident because this will help you sound more persuasive.

Activity 7

a Deliver your speech to a group of your peers, a teacher or to the whole class.

b Afterwards, evaluate how well you did in the activities listed below. Give yourself a score from 1 to 3 for each activity, where 1 = Poor ('I could have put in more effort'); 2 = Satisfactory ('I did OK but I can do better next time'); 3 = Great ('I nailed it').
   - Sustainable holiday planning
   - Use of persuasive techniques
   - Speech rehearsal
   - Delivery of speech

c Set yourself two targets for next time.

> ✅ **Tip**
>
> If you get nervous when talking in front of an audience, the advice below should help.
> 1. Be prepared. Do your research and practise your speech.
> 2. Practise again! The more you practise, the less nervous you will get.
> 3. Just before you speak, take slow, deep breaths. Visualise yourself standing up and smiling and doing well.
> 4. Don't rush! If you go too fast, you are more likely to stumble.

151

3: Journeys and discoveries

3.7 Why take a risk?

In this unit, you will:
- learn to recognise the effect of a writer's choice of techniques in a piece of travel writing
- explore how the structure of a piece of travel writing creates excitement
- write an article about a travel adventure.

What's the big idea?

Have you ever taken a calculated risk, just for the thrill of it? Abseiling, deep-sea diving, sky-diving, zooming down a half pipe – these are all popular activities that present a degree of physical danger and make the human body react in a particular way. Stress and excitement cause adrenaline to rush through the body, making the heart beat faster, increasing energy and the ability to move quickly. Writers convey this excitement in adventure travel writing.

In this unit, you will read about just such a travel adventure and then write about one.

Activity 1

a What do you know about the extreme travel activities below?

| hot-air balloon flight | wild camping | desert sand-surfing |

| touring the inside of a volcano | swimming with dolphins |

| glacier hunting | mountain climbing | whitewater rafting |

b What features do you think might be included in extreme travel writing?

c Which techniques do you think writers might use to make something sound dangerous or frightening?

Did you know?

The Seven Wonders of the Natural World are usually listed as: Victoria Falls, the Northern Lights, Rio de Janeiro Harbour, the Grand Canyon, Mount Everest, Paricutin and the Great Barrier Reef.

On a trip to Africa, writer Deborah O'Donoghue visited Victoria Falls, which forms the border between Zambia and Zimbabwe and is one of the Seven Natural Wonders of the World.

'Bungee at Victoria Falls: The Day the Void Came for Me' by Deborah O'Donoghue

We arrived there, at Mosi-oa-Tunya ('The Smoke that Thunders') or Victoria Falls in the afternoon, entering on the Zambian side of the park. It was a warm winter day, in August's medium-to-high-water season. This meant you could glimpse the steep, jagged rock faces of the gorge but there was still plenty enough water crashing over the cliff edge to fill the air with droplets which look like rising smoke – **hence** the Sotho language name.

Surrounded by rainbows and mist, we crossed Knife Edge, a narrow structure near the precipice taking visitors almost as close as they can get to the Falls. The greatest waterfall on Earth plummeted beside us. Then we had some free time. I wandered in awe through the park for a while before **reconvening** with the others at Gorilla Head Viewpoint, where sure enough there is a rock that looks like a gorilla's head, as well as a spectacular view over the river and the Victoria Falls Bridge. Constructed in Great Britain and assembled on site in 1905, the bridge is an **audacious** single span of steel, 128 metres above the river, and the only rail link between Zambia and Zimbabwe.

There was a strange disquiet among our small group as I re-joined. I realised they were watching people throw themselves off the railway bridge, with rope attached. Bungee-jumpers. I shook my head in disbelief. *Who were these idiots? What would possess you to do something like that?* I was not fond of heights. My knees had trembled a little earlier, simply crossing Knife Edge overlooking the eastern edge of the **cataracts**. There was no way I would ever be able to bungee-jump. Would I?

I'd never thought of myself as a risk-taker. I didn't chase adrenaline-highs or seek out danger. But as I stood looking at the tiny figures jumping and dangling from a rope attached to a railway bridge 128 metres above the thundering Zambezi River, my heart began to pound in my chest. They must be insane, I thought. The next thing forming inside me wasn't a thought or even a feeling; it was just something I knew.

I am going to do that too.

---

hence – for this reason
reconvening – meeting again

audacious – daring, shocking
cataracts – large, steep waterfalls

3: Journeys and discoveries

⭐ Boosting your vocabulary

Writers choose their words carefully. The activity below focuses on some key vocabulary in the source text, which has been highlighted on page 153.

Activity 2

a Find each of the words below in the text and read its definition.

  glimpse (see for a moment)   spectacular (very impressive)

  fond (keen, having warm feelings)

  Use each word in a sentence of your own.

b Look at the words below in the text on p153. How do the words add more drama and a sense of adventure to the sentences they appear in? Think about the impact of the sentences without these descriptions.

  plummeted   dangling   thundering

⬆ Stretch yourself

Write a paragraph to explain how the writer's choice of words has created a sense of excitement in the article.

💡 Building your knowledge

In this piece of travel writing, the author builds up to the moment of her decision to jump, using a number of techniques to create a sense of excitement:

- repeated references to the dramatic setting, e.g. 'cliff edge', '128 metres above',
- verbs to create action and drama, e.g. 'crashing', 'plummeted'
- noun phrases to inspire awe, e.g. 'the steep, jagged rock faces of the gorge', 'an audacious single span of steel'
- questions and reflections, e.g. 'I shook my head in disbelief,' 'Would I?'
- one-sentence paragraph for dramatic effect, e.g. 'I am going to do that too.'.

The writer uses these techniques to describe the awe and wonder of the physical landscape and to chart her inner thoughts, fears and reflections as she watches others complete the task, and wonders whether or not she can do it too.

3.7: Why take a risk?

Activity 3

a   Match each of the paragraph summaries below to the correct paragraph in the extract on p153.

| Account of watching others take on the challenge | Focus on arriving at the location and journey | Exploration of the writer's inner thoughts and fears | Description of the physcial landscape |

b   How does the excitement build through the article? Think about the content of each paragraph.

Activity 4

Look at each technique listed in the table below and how it helps to create the sense of excitement. Complete a table like the one below. Find further examples of each feature and explore its impact on the reader.

Technique	Further examples	How does it impact the reader?
Verbs to create action and drama	'crashing'	
Noun phrases to inspire awe		
Questions and reflections that show the author's fear		

155

3: Journeys and discoveries

You are going to write an article for a travel website, in which you describe an amazing travel adventure and the build-up to your decision to have a go – or not.

Activity 5

a Start by choosing the travel adventure you want to write about. Use the ideas on page 152 and the photos of abseiling, extreme wheelchair downhill riding and endurance racing **on this page** to help you.

b Talk to a partner about your choice and jot down ideas against each of the prompts below. You may need to do some research.
- What will the landscape of your chosen challenge be like?
- What are the potential thrills and dangers?
- Imagine a few people are waiting for or already doing the activity – what behaviours will they be showing and why?
- What would cause you to hesitate before the activity? What will make you do it? Or not?

c Create a plan for what content you'll cover in each paragraph of your writing. Use the extract on p153 and your answers to activity 3 to help you plan.

156

3.7: Why take a risk?

Putting it all together

Activity 6

a Write an article to be published on a travel website in which you describe an adrenaline-fuelled travel experience and the build-up to your decision to have a go – or not. Use your answers from activities 3–5 to help you.

You must:
- describe the location for the adventure
- build up the sense of excitement over a number of paragraphs
- reveal your feelings and how they change
- end by revealing your decision.

b When you have finished, read your work aloud and then write a short reflection. Comment on:
- what you enjoyed about this piece of writing
- what was challenging about this piece of writing
- what techniques you used successfully, such as noun phrases for the landscape or repetition to emphasise something about the location
- any techniques you could use better next time
- what you are proud of in this piece of writing.

Stretch yourself

When your article is complete, write a paragraph to explain how your choice of words creates excitement in the reader.

3: Journeys and discoveries

3.8 Can journeys tell stories?

In this unit, you will:
- learn about the conventions of autobiographical writing
- learn how to structure an analytical response
- write about a literary text using a formal, analytical style.

What's the big idea?

Travel writing and autobiography share many features. Travel writers often reveal details about their lives when they are writing about journeys and places; autobiographical writing often includes accounts of significant journeys.

In this unit, you will read an extract from an autobiography that describes aspects of an important journey, analyse the writer's approach and comment on how it impacts on the reader.

Activity 1

An autobiography is the story of a person's life written by the person themselves.

a Do you know any autobiographies? Think about books written by sports people, celebrities and politicians.

b Why do you think people like to read autobiographies?

In the extracts from her autobiography on pages 159 and 160 – written as a series of poems – Jacqueline Woodson describes the journey her mother took from her home in Ohio to her parents' home in South Carolina. Jacqueline Woodson was a baby at the time and her father resented the visits.

3.8: Can journeys tell stories?

Extract 1 from *Brown Girl Dreaming* by Jacqueline Woodson

journey

You can keep your South, my father says.
The way they treated us down there,
I got your mama out as quick as I could.
Brought her right up here to **Ohio**.
Told her there's never gonna be a Woodson
that sits in the back of the bus.
Never gonna be a Woodson that has to
Yes sir and No sir white people.
Never gonna be a Woodson made to look down
at the ground.

All you kids are stronger than that, my father says.
All you Woodson kids deserve to be
as good as you already are.

Yes sirree, Bob, my father says.
You can keep your **South Carolina**.

Ohio – a northern state in the USA

Yes sirree, Bob – colloquial expression meaning 'yes, absolutely'

South Carolina – a southern state in the USA

Extract 2 from *Brown Girl Dreaming* by Jacqueline Woodson

greenville, south carolina, 1963

On the bus, my mother moves with us to the back.
It is 1963
in South Carolina.
Too dangerous to sit closer to the front
            and dare the driver
to make her move. Not with us. Not now.
Me in her arms all of three months old. My sister
and brother squeezed into the seat beside her. White
shirt, tie, and my brother's head shaved clean.
        My sister's braids
white ribboned.

Sit up straight, my mother says.
She tells my brother to take his fingers
        out of his mouth.
They do what is asked of them.
Although they don't know why they have to.
This isn't Ohio, my mother says,
        as though we understand.
Her mouth a small lipsticked dash, her back
sharp as a line. DO NOT CROSS!
COLOREDS TO THE BACK!
Step off the curb if a white person comes toward you
don't look them in the eye. Yes sir. No sir.
        My apologies.
Her eyes straight ahead, my mother
is miles away from here.

Then her mouth softens, her hand moves gently
over my brother's warm head. He is three years old,
his wide eyes open to the world, his too-big ears
already listening. *We're as good as anybody*,
my mother whispers.

As good as anybody.

Too dangerous to sit closer to the front and dare the driver to make her move - In 1955, Rosa Parks, a Black resident of Montgomery in Alabama, was asked to move seats to make room for a white man. She refused, sparking a bus boycott and a series of protests.

coloreds – dated and offensive term for Black people

3: Journeys and discoveries

Extract 3 from *Brown Girl Dreaming* by Jacqueline Woodson

home

Soon...
We are near my other grandparents' house,
    small red stone,
    immense yard surrounding it.
5   Hall Street.
A front porch swing thirsty for oil.
A pot of azaleas blooming.
A pine tree.
Red dirt **wafting** up
10 around my mother's newly polished shoes.

Welcome home, my grandparents say.
    Their warm brown
arms around us. A white handkerchief,
    embroidered with blue
15 to wipe away my mother's tears. And me,
the new baby, set deep
inside this love.

Red dirt – South Carolina is well-known for red soil, caused by the bedrock of iron-rich clay

★ Boosting your vocabulary

Writers choose their words carefully. The activities below focuses on some key vocabulary in the source text, which has been highlighted above.

Activity 2

a   Complete each sentence using one of the highlighted words from the text:
    i   The smell of dinner was _____ through the house.
    ii The cushions were _____ with red flowers.
    iii They had only just started work – there was still an _____ amount to do.

b   Come up with your own definition of each word.

3.8: Can journeys tell stories?

> **Building your knowledge**

Autobiographical writing tells the story of the writer's life. It is usually:
- written in the first person (using I, we and me)
- written in the past tense (e.g. I travelled..., we ran...)
- presented in **chronological** order (e.g. autobiographies might start by exploring the writer's childhood, before moving on to adulthood)
- focused on key experiences that reveal something about the writer.

A lot of travel writing has similar characteristics.

> **Key term**
>
> **chronological** arranged in the order in which things happened
>
> **metaphor** a comparison that says one thing *is* something else, e.g. *Amy was a rock*

Activity 3

a Find examples of the features above in the extracts on p159–160.

b Autobiographical texts are usually written in prose (written in sentences and paragraphs). Why do you think the writer choose to write her autobiography as a series of poems?

You are going to comment on the extracts, explaining how the writer's choices convey meaning and impact on the reader.

Activity 4

While autobiographies and travel writing are both non-fiction, they often include figurative language and other features that you might expect to find in fiction texts. One student noted some key features of the extracts on pages 159–160
Find evidence from the text to match each feature.

Direct speech – allows readers to hear the voices of significant people	Minor sentences – convey emphasis and highlight key points
Clear and vivid details – create a strong image of important moments	Colloquial language – conveys the authentic voice and attitude of key people
Exclamation marks – emphasise a commanding tone	Simile / **metaphor** – create striking comparisons

Factual information – provides relevant social and historical context

> **Stretch yourself**
>
> Why do you think an autobiography might focus on journeys? Think about what you've learned about physical and inner journeys in units 1–3.

161

3: Journeys and discoveries

In activity 6 you're going to write an answer to the following question:

> How does Jacqueline Woodson's writing about an important journey impact on the reader?

To craft an analytical response, you'll need to:

- use formal language (e.g. 'arrives at their destination' instead of 'gets home')
- use cohesive devices (e.g. 'Another significant moment is…', 'This could be…')
- introduce your point in the first sentence of each paragraph (e.g. 'There are several important moments in the text')
- include evidence from the text to support your point – this could be a reference to something that happens in the text or an **embedded quotation** (e.g. 'the writer describes "red dirt wafting up" over her mother's shoes')
- make it clear what the impact or significance of the evidence is – what does it suggest or reveal about the character, for example?

Activity 5

Focusing on one of the key features you explored in activity 4, write a paragraph to comment on its impact on the reader. Use what you've learned above to help you craft your response.

3.8: Can journeys tell stories?

Putting it all together

Activity 6

Using your answers from activity 4 and 5 to help you, write four to five paragraphs in answer to the question below.

> How does Jacqueline Woodson's writing about an important journey impact on the reader?

a Plan your paragraphs. You could create a mind map and number the points, or make a list of paragraph headings with two or three bullets under each to remind you what to include.

b Decide what evidence from the text (quotations) you are going to use to back up your ideas.

c Write the first two or three paragraphs of your answer and then stop to check how your work is going.
  - Are you referring to the key features of the text, like the ones you explored on page 161 and in activity 4?
  - Is your language formal?
  - Are you linking your ideas together with cohesive devices?
  - Are you referring to key features?
  - Are you using quotations?

d Complete your answer and then reflect on your work. Consider these questions:
  - What have I done well?
  - What can I improve?
  - What help do I need?

🔑 Key terms

embedded quotation
when a word or phrase from the text is used in a sentence about the text

Key terms glossary

abstract existing as an idea but not having a physical reality

abstract noun a noun that refers to an idea, quality or emotion, rather than a solid object, e.g. *happiness, truth, freedom*

adjectival phrase a phrase that describe a person or thing

adjective a word that describes a noun

adverb a word that you use with a verb, adjective or other adverb that tells you how, when or where something happened

adverbial a word or phrase that explains how, where or when something happened, or how ideas relate to one another

alliteration using the same letter or sound at the beginning of several words for special effect

anecdote a short or entertaining story about real people or events

antagonist main opponent

antonym a word that has the opposite meaning of a particular word

archaic old-fashioned, from a different historical time

audience the people or person for whom a text is written or performed

autobiographical based on the writer's life

bilingual able to speak two languages

byline a line at the beginning or end of a newspaper or magazine article that gives the writer's name

character a person in a drama or story

characterisation the methods an author uses to create a character, e.g. describing how they look, the use of dialogue or showing how they treat others

chronological arranged in the order in which things happened

cliffhanger an exciting event at the end of a chapter, leaving the reader anxious and eager to know what happens next

climax when the action is at its most exciting or interesting

code-switching moving between different levels of formality in language, e.g. between Standard English and non-standard English.

cohesive device a word or phrase that links ideas together, e.g. *at the beginning, however, although*

colloquial language informal words or phrases that are suitable for ordinary conversation, rather than formal speech or writing

coming-of-age story a story in which characters experience things that teach them about adulthood

commentary a written explanation or discussion

compare judge how two or more things are similar and different

compound noun a word that is made up of two or more other words. Some compound words have hyphens, but not all, e.g. *ear-splitting, suitcase, hedgehog*

conflict a struggle or disagreement between people

conjunction a linking word, e.g. *if, and, but*

connective a general term for a word or phrase that helps link information

connotation an idea or feeling linked to a word, as well as its main meaning

context the time, place and influences on a text from when it was written, and from when it is read, which shape our understanding of the text; also, the words that come before and after a particular word or phrase and help to clarify its meaning

contrast difference between two or more things; also, to compare to show a difference

convention a typical feature you find in a particular genre

debate to have a formal discussion in which opposite views on a subject are heard fairly

dialect a form of a language linked to a specific region, e.g. Geordie in Newcastle upon Tyne

dialogue words spoken by characters

direct address addressing the reader as you

drama a play written for performance on stage or to be listened to

editorial a newspaper article expressing a writer's opinion

ellipsis three dots (…) used to show a pause or to indicate that a word or words have been left out

embedded quotation when a word or phrase from the text is used in a sentence about the text

emotive language word choices that create a strong emotional reaction in the reader

empathy the ability to understand and share in someone else's feelings

evidence and statistics data and facts

explicit stating something openly and exactly

fantasy an imaginary story that is not based on reality

fiction a narrative that is imaginary or invented

figurative language words or phrases with a meaning that is different from the literal meaning

first-person narrative a story told by someone as if they were involved in the events themselves, using first-person pronouns, e.g. *I* and *we*

first-person plural pronoun we and us are ways of speaking in the first person about more than one person

fluency speaking with a smooth flow, without hesitating

foreshadowing a technique that gives a hint of something that will develop later

form the organisation of writing in a particular way, e.g. a letter or a poem

genre a type of story, e.g. *horror, romance, adventure, science fiction*

gesture using your hands to indicate meaning, e.g. to help emphasise certain points

headline the title of a news article printed in large letters

implicit not stated directly, but suggested or hinted at

inciting incident the event that sets up the action for the rest of the story

infer to work something out from what is seen, said or done, even though it is not stated directly

internal monologue inner speech (in someone's head)

Key terms glossary

juvenile linked to young people

metaphor a comparison that says one thing is something else, e.g. *Amy was a rock*

minor sentence sometimes known as a sentence fragment, a sentence without a main verb or subject

modal verb a verb that works with another verb to show that something needs to happen or might possibly happen, e.g. *must, shall, will, should, would, can, could, may* and *might*

monologue a speech by one character

mythical from a myth, a traditional story that often includes supernatural beings

narrative a story or account of connected events

narrative voice the perspective (viewpoint) from which a story is told, and the style in which it is told

narrator a person who tells a story, especially in a book, play or film

nemesis an enemy or competitor that cannot be avoided

non-fiction real events or factual information

non-narrative information that is not part of a sequence of events

non-standard English an informal version of English, often used with family and friends, including slang and regional variations

noun phrase a noun plus information before and/or after the noun

objective not influenced by personal feeling or opinion

onomatopoeia words that imitate or suggest what they stand for, e.g. *cuckoo, sizzle*

pace the speed at which someone moves or something happens

pathetic fallacy giving emotions to something non-human in the natural world to reflect a character's feelings or situation

persuasive making you want to do or believe something

poetry a piece of writing often arranged in short lines and stanzas, following a pattern of sounds, and expressing feelings and ideas with great imagination

prefix a word or group of letters placed in front of another word to add to or change its meaning

prepositional phrase a phrase that begins with a preposition (e.g. *between, near, by, beyond*) and tells the reader about location and place

pronoun a word used instead of a noun or noun phrase, e.g. *he, it, they*

prose written language in its ordinary form, rather than poetry or drama

protagonist main character

purpose the reason that a text is written

quotation a word or phrase from a text

recital a performance

register the manner of speaking or writing, which can range between formal and informal

repetition using the same word or phrase more than once

rhetorical question a question asked for dramatic effect and not intended to get an answer

rhyme using the same sound to end words, particularly at the ends of lines

rhythm the pattern of beats in a line of music or poetry

root the core of a word that has meaning. It may or may not be a complete word

scanning reading quickly to find something specific

sensationalist presented in a deliberate way to stir up excitement and interest

setting where the action takes place

simile a comparison of one thing to another, using *as* or *like*, e.g. *He swam like a fish*

stage direction an instruction to an actor about movement or expression, or a description of a sound effect

Standard English a widely recognised formal version of English, not linked to any region, but used in schools, exams, official publications and in public announcements

standfirst a sentence or two beneath a headline, but before the main body of an article, which introduces what follows

stanza a group of lines in a poem with a line space before and after it

structural feature a feature used by a writer to give a text its overall shape

subject the person or thing that does the verb, e.g. *the boy eats, tigers prowl, the building exists*

subjective influenced by personal feeling or opinion

suffix a word or group of letters placed at the end of another word or root to add to or change its meaning

suspense a feeling of anxious uncertainty while waiting for something to happen or become known

synonym a word or phrase that means the same, or almost the same, as another word or phrase

synthesise to combine separate parts into something new

technical information specialised words or phrases

tension a feeling of being on edge with nerves stretched tight

text any form of written material

third-person narrative a story told by someone who was not involved in the events themselves, using third-person pronouns, e.g. *he, she, they*

tone the writer's feeling or attitude expressed towards their subject; in fiction it can also reflect a character's feelings and personality

transcript a written record of spoken words

travel writing writing produced during or after a journey, describing it in order to inform and/or entertain readers

tricolon a pattern of three words or phrases grouped together to be memorable and have impact

unreliable narrator a narrator who may or may not prove to be trustworthy, either intentionally or otherwise

verb a word or group of words that express an action, event or state, e.g. *the boy eats, tigers prowl, the building exists*

Boosting your vocabulary glossary

activists *(noun)* people who take action to bring about change, especially in politics

alien *(adjective)* unnatural or unfamiliar

anti-empire *(adjective)* against an empire

bodegas *(noun)* small corner shops or local stores

brutality *(noun)* cruelty and violence

campus *(noun)* the grounds and buildings of a university or college

challenge *(noun)* a task or activity that is new and exciting but also difficult

chaos *(noun)* great disorder

clammy *(adjective)* damp and slimy

cold *(adjective)* not friendly or loving

coldly *(adverb)* in an unfriendly or distant way

confined *(verb)* kept within limits; restricted

consequences *(noun)* things that happen as the result of an event or action

convention *(noun)* a typical feature you find in a particular genre

damp *(adjective)* slightly wet; not quite dry

dangling *(verb)* swinging or hanging loosely

delinquency *(noun)* minor crime, especially by young people

demonising *(verb)* portraying someone as being evil or dangerous

destruction *(noun)* destroying something or being destroyed

detective *(noun)* a person, especially a police officer, who investigates crimes

devastated *(adjective)* overwhelmed with shock or grief

discovery *(noun)*
(1) discovering something or being discovered
(2) something that is discovered

distant *(adjective)* not friendly; not sociable

distraught *(adjective)* greatly upset by worry or distress

doubt *(verb)* to feel unsure or undecided about something

drips *(noun)* liquid falling in drops

embroidered *(adjective)* cloth that has been decorated with sewing designs

empire *(noun)* a group of countries controlled by one person or government

equal *(adjective)* the same in amount, size or value

equality *(noun)* the state of being equal

expedition *(noun)* a journey or voyage made in order to do something

experience *(noun)* something that has happened to you

exposition *(noun)* a passage in a text that introduces the reader to characters and background events

fissures *(noun)* narrow openings made where something splits or separates

fragmented *(adjective)* broken up into small pieces

gentle *(adjective)* mild or kind; not rough

gleam *(noun)* a beam or ray of soft light, often one that comes and goes

glimpse *(verb)* to see something briefly

graciously *(adverb)* generously and pleasantly

guilt *(noun)* an unpleasant feeling when you have done wrong or are to blame for something

heir *(noun)* a person who inherits money or a title

honour *(noun)* something a person is proud to do

immense *(adjective)* extremely large or great; huge

impatient *(adjective)* not patient or tolerant

impressionable *(adjective)* easily influenced or affected

incredibly *(adverb)* impossible to believe

inquisitive *(adjective)* always asking questions or trying to find out things

intrigue *(verb)* to interest someone very much and make them curious

intriguing *(adjective)* very interesting to someone

investigation *(noun)* a careful search for information about something

jeopardy *(noun)* danger of harm or failure

lashing *(verb)* raining heavily

laundromats *(noun)* (American spelling) places fitted with washing machines that people pay to use

loathed *(verb)* greatly hated

melancholy *(adjective)* sad, gloomy

miraculously *(adverb)* wonderfully or unexpectedly

mist *(noun)* damp, cloudy air near the ground

mizzling *(adjective)* raining in very fine droplets; drizzling

motive *(noun)* what makes a person do something

murder *(verb)* to kill a person unlawfully and deliberately

mystery *(noun)* something that cannot be explained or understood; something puzzling

Boosting your vocabulary glossary

narrow-minded *(adjective)* unwilling to accept other people's beliefs and ways

obsessed *(verb)* to be obsessed with something is to be continually thinking about it

ought *(modal verb)* used to show what you should or must do

painfully *(adverb)* in a way that causes pain

pattered *(verb)* made light, tapping sounds

pitiless *(adjective)* showing no pity; harsh or cruel

plummeted *(verb)* dropped downwards quickly

power *(noun)*
  (1) strength or energy
  (2) the ability to do something

prism *(noun)* a glass prism that breaks up light into the colours of the rainbow

prodigious *(adjective)* remarkably large or impressive

profoundly *(adverb)* very deeply or intensely

quest *(noun)* a long search for something

rage *(noun)* great or violent anger

reasoning *(verb)* using your ability to think and draw conclusions

reflects *(verb)* sends back light, heat or sound from a surface

reigns *(verb)* to be the most noticeable or important thing

reputation *(noun)* the opinion that is generally held about a person or thing

resolution *(noun)* the last part of a story where we find out how the story comes to an end and how difficulties are sorted out

rich *(adjective)* rich food contains a lot of fat, butter or eggs

routine *(noun)* a regular way of doing things

screaming *(verb)* letting out a loud cry of pain, fear, anger or excitement

shame *(noun)* a feeling of great sorrow or guilt because you have done wrong

silence *(noun)* absence of sound

slabs *(noun)* thick, flat pieces

soaked *(verb)* made a person or thing very wet

sobbed *(verb)* cried, took sharp breaths

solitary confinement *(noun)* a form of punishment in which a prisoner is kept alone in a cell and not allowed to see other people

special *(adjective)* not ordinary or usual

spectacular *(adjective)* impressive or striking

splashed *(verb)* made liquid fly about in drops

stimulate *(verb)* to make someone excited or enthusiastic

stings *(verb)* wounds or hurts someone with a sting

straggly *(adjective)* growing or spreading untidily

stung *(verb)* wounded or hurt someone with a sting

supernatural *(adjective)* not belonging to the natural world or having a natural explanation

suspects *(noun)* people who are suspected of a crime or doing something wrong

sustainable *(adjective)* using natural products and energy in a way that does not harm the environment

taboo *(noun)* a custom that you should avoid doing or talking about a particular thing because it might offend or embarrass other people

terrified *(adjective)* very afraid

terrorists *(noun)* people who use violence for political purposes

thrill *(noun)* a feeling of great excitement or pleasure

thundering *(verb)* making the noise of thunder or a noise like thunder

tossing *(verb)* moving relentlessly or unevenly from side to side

tragedy *(noun)* a very sad or distressing event

trickle *(noun)* a slow movement or flow

vandals *(noun)* people who deliberately break or damage things, especially public property

vibrant *(adjective)* vibrant colours are bright and strong

vulnerable *(adjective)* easily able to be hurt or harmed or attacked

wafting *(verb)* floating gently through the air

writhing *(verb)* twisting your body about because of pain or discomfort

yobs *(noun)* (informal) bad-mannered or aggressive young people

youths *(noun)* young people

OXFORD
UNIVERSITY PRESS

Great Clarendon Street, Oxford, OX2 6DP, United Kingdom

Oxford University Press is a department of the University of Oxford. It furthers the University's objective of excellence in research, scholarship, and education by publishing worldwide. Oxford is a registered trade mark of Oxford University Press in the UK and in certain other countries.

© Oxford University Press 2023

The moral rights of the authors have been asserted

First published in 2023

All rights reserved. No part of this publication may be reproduced, stored in a retrieval system, or transmitted, in any form or by any means, without the prior permission in writing of Oxford University Press, or as expressly permitted by law, by licence or under terms agreed with the appropriate reprographics rights organization. Enquiries concerning reproduction outside the scope of the above should be sent to the Rights Department, Oxford University Press, at the address above.

You must not circulate this work in any other form and you must impose this same condition on any acquirer

British Library Cataloguing in Publication Data
Data available

978-1-38-203327-5
978-1-38-203328-2 (ebook)

10 9 8 7 6 5 4 3 2 1

Paper used in the production of this book is a natural, recyclable product made from wood grown in sustainable forests.

The manufacturing process conforms to the environmental regulations of the country of origin.

Printed in Great Britain by Bell and Bain Ltd., Glasgow.

Acknowledgements

The publisher would like to thank the following for permissions to use copyright material:

Chimamanda Ngozi Adichie: 'The Danger of the Single Story' by Chimamanda Ngozi Adichie. Copyright © 2014, Chimamanda Ngozi Adichie, used by permission of The Wylie Agency (UK) Limited.

Air Ambulance: Extract from Air Ambulance handout - 'See how your support makes a difference'. Copyright © 2022 The Air Ambulance Service. Used with permission.

Grace Blair: Extract from '4 Reasons We Love Binging Crime Shows' published in Psychology Today, February 18, 2021. Copyright © Psychology Today. Used with permission.

Gemma Bowes: Extracts from the article '20 of the best sustainable holidays in Europe for 2020' written by Gemma Bowes, pub 26/12/2019' The Guardian. Used by permission from Guardian News & Media Limited.

Jessie Burton: Extract from Medusa: A 'beautiful and profound retelling of Medusa's story by Jessie Burton 2021, Bloomsbury Publishing PLC. Copyright © 2021 Jessie Burton. Used by permission from Bloomsbury Publishing PLC.

Helena Dixon: Extract from Cover blurb for Murder at the Dolphin Hotel by Helena Dixon (2019), Bookouture. Copyright © 2019 Helena Dixon. Used with permission from Bookouture.

Daphne Du Maurier: Extracts from Jamaica Inn by Daphne Du Maurier, 2003, Virago. Copyright © 2003 Daphne Du Maurier. Used by permission from Curtis Brown.

Carol Ann Duffy: Poem 'Stealing' by Carol Ann Duffy 1987. Copyright © Carol Ann Duffy. Reproduced by permission of the author c/o Rogers, Coleridge & White Ltd., 20 Powis Mews, London W11 1JN

Ally Fogg: Extract from the article 'Who should get credit for declining youth crime? Young people of course' by Ally Fogg, 16 May 2014; published by The Independent. Used by permission from Independent Digital News and Media Limited.

Sagar Garg: Poem 'Guilty Conscience' by Sagar Garg. Copyright © 2017 Sagar Garg. Used with permission from the author.

Tavi Gevinson: Extract from 'How to Not Care What Other People Think of You'. Copyright © 2011–2018 Rookie. Used with permission.

Fleur Hitchcock: Extract from Murder in Midwinter by Fleur Hitchcock (2016), published by Nosy Crow. Copyright © 2016 Fleur Hitchcock. Used with permission from Nosy Crow Limited.

Alastair Humphreys: Extract from 'Alastair Humphreys - Living Adventurously – America'. Copyright © Alastair Humphreys. Used by permission from David Higham Associates.

Sharna Jackson: Extract from Cover blurb for High Rise Mystery by Sharna Jackson (2019), Knights of Media. Copyright © 2019 Sharna Jackson. Used with permission from Knights of Limited.

Stephen Kelman: Extract from the book Pigeon English by Stephen Kelman 2015. Copyright © Stephen Kelman. Reprinted by permission from Bloomsbury Publishing Plc.

Stephen King: Extract from The Body by Stephen King 2021, Hodder and Stoughton. Copyright © 2021 Stephen King. Reproduced with permission of the Licensor through PLSclear.

C.S. Lewis: Extract from The Lion, the Witch and the Wardrobe by C.S. Lewis copyright © C.S. Lewis Pte. Ltd. 1950. Reprinted by permission from The CS Lewis Company Ltd.

Laura Mowat: Extract from the article – 'Grown men in tears as DISGUSTING yobs DESTROY beloved model railway exhibition for fun' written by Laura Mowat and published by Express Newspaper. Copyright ©2023 Express Newspapers. Reprinted by permission from Reach Licensing/mirrorpix.

No Such Thing Production: Transcript from Episode 9, Scene 1 of 'Here Be Dragons' by Jordan Cobb. Copyright © 2018 by No Such Thing Productions. Used by permission.

Deborah O'Donoghue: Extract from the article – 'Bungee at Victoria Falls: The Day the Void Came for Me' written by Deborah O'Donoghue; 18th Nov. 2020, Travel Tomorrow. Used by permission from the author.

Wang Ping: Poem 'Things We Carry on the Sea' by Wang Ping. Originally published in New American Poetry. Copyright © 2018 by Wang Ping. Used by permission from Hanging Loose Press.

Shukria Rezaei: Poem 'I Want a Poem'. Copyright © Shukria Rezaei. Used by permission of the author.

Michael Romero: Extract from the article – 'A Day in the Life of a Prisoner' by Michael Romero, published in Pen America, November 16, 2012. Copyright © 2012 Michael Romero. Used with permission from the author.

Kim Slater: Extract from Smart: A Mysterious Crime, a Different Detective by Kim Slater (2014), Macmillan Children's Books. Copyright © 2014 Kim Slater. Used with permission from Macmillan Children's Books.

Robin Stevens: Extract from Cover blurb for Arsenic for Tea: A Murder Most Unladylike Mystery by Robin Stevens (2016), Penguin. Copyright © 2016 Robin Stevens.

Jacqueline Woodson: Poems 'greenville, south carolina, 1963'; 'journey'; 'home' from Brown Girl Dreaming by Jacqueline Woodson, Penguin. Copyright © 2020 Jacqueline Woodson.

Malala Yousafzai: Transcript of speech given by Malala Yousafzai (Co-Founder of Malala Fund & Nobel Laureate) to the UN Youth Assembly. Copyright © Malala Yousafzai. Used by permission from United Talent Agency, LLC.

Benjamin Zephaniah: Extract from Talking Turkeys by Benjamin Zephaniah, Penguin, 1994. Copyright © 1994 Benjamin Zephaniah.

Benjamin Zephaniah: Extract from Too Black, Too Strong (Bloodaxe Books, 2001). Reproduced with permission of Bloodaxe Books. www.bloodaxebooks.com

Photos: Throughout: schab/Shutterstock; **p8(1)**: Sk_Advance studio / Shutterstock; p8(1, inset): totally out/Shutterstock; **p8(2)**: Justin Kase ztwoz / Alamy Stock Photo; **p9(3)**: Ceri Breeze/Shutterstock; **p9(4)**: Radu Bercan / Shutterstock; **p9(5)**: Heritage Image Partnership Ltd / Alamy Stock Photo; **p9(6)**: Patti McConville / Alamy Stock Photo; **p13**: Diego Thomazini / Shutterstock; pp14/15(bkg): StefanRenner / Shutterstock; **p15**: Heritage Image Partnership Ltd / Alamy Stock Photo; **p17**: Contributor / NBCUniversal /NBC / Getty Images; **p19**: Madlen/Shutterstock; **p20**: Mila Drumeva / Shutterstock; **p21**: Neda.tm / Shutterstock; **pp22/23**: Amoret Tanner / Alamy Stock Photo; **pp24/25**: worldclassphoto / Shutterstock; **p27**: DarwelPics / Alamy Stock Photo; **p28**: Justin Kase z12z / Alamy Stock Photo; **p30**: Donald Cooper / Photostage; **p33**: Martin Bache / Alamy Stock Photo; **p35**: Chris K Horne / Shutterstock; **p37**: OLAYOLA / Alamy Stock Photo; **p39**: Donald Cooper / Photostage; **p40**: AF Fotografie / Alamy Stock Photo; **p43**: Jeff Morgan 04 / Alamy Stock Photo; **p45**: Jonny White / Alamy Stock Photo; **p46(tl)**: Eva Morales; **p46(tl)**: Krakenimages.com / Shutterstock; **p46(tl)**: Ros Kavanagh-VIEW / Alamy Stock Photo; **p46(tr)**: Becka Moor; **p46(bl)**: Binny Talib; **p46(bm)**: Paula Bowles; **p46(br)**: Pete Williamson; **p50**: Jeff Morgan 16 / Alamy Stock Photo; **p52**: Monkey Business Images / Shutterstock; **p53**: Mike Goldwater / Alamy Stock Photo; **pp54/55**: Drop of Light / Shutterstock; **p56**: Ink Drop / Shutterstock; **p57**: Newscom / Alamy Stock Photo; **p58**: imageBROKER / Alamy Stock Photo; **p59**: View Factor Images / Shutterstock; **p60(1)**: New Africa / Shutterstock; **p60(2)**: Marjorie Kamys Cotera / Bob Daemmrich Photography / Alamy Stock Photo; **p61(3)**: Sergii Gnatiuk / Shutterstock; **p61(4)**: Gorodenkoff / Shutterstock; **p61(5)**: Image Source / Alamy Stock Photo; **p61(6)**: Daniel Samray / Shutterstock; **p64**: steeve-x-art / Alamy Stock Photo; **p67(l)**: Columbia Pictures / Photo 12 / Alamy Stock Photo; **p67(r)**: Album / Alamy Stock Photo; **p68**: RMC42 / Shutterstock; **p70**: Library of Congress Prints and Photographs Division; **p71**: PytyCzech / iStock / Getty Images Plus / Getty Images; **p72**: Public Domain; **p73**: Margo Alexa / Shutterstock; **p74**: MarioGuti / iStock / Getty Images Plus / Getty Images; **p78**: Jenny Matthews / Alamy Stock Photo; **p80**: pikselstock / Shutterstock; **p81**: Dietmar Rauscher / Alamy Stock Photo; **p82**: IR Stone / Shutterstock; **p84**: Adrian Sherratt / Alamy Stock Photo; **p87**: SolStock / E+ / Getty Images; **p89**: SWNS; **p90**: DedMityay / Shutterstock; **p92**: Billion Photos / Shutterstock; **p95**: Elena Rostunova / Shutterstock; **p96**: woff / Shutterstock; **p98**: Dayday24 / Alamy Stock Photo; **pp100/101**: Joseph Sohm / Shutterstock; **p102**: Trinity Mirror / Mirrorpix / Alamy Stock Photo; **p103**: AUL LOEB / AFP via Getty Images; **p105**: Alex Walker / Moment / Getty Images; **pp106/107**: Toby Howard / Shutterstock; **p108**: AS photostudio / Shutterstock; **pp110/111**: rightclickstudios / Shutterstock; **p112(1)**: Thana Prasongsin / Moment / Getty Images; **p112(2)**: Nick Fox / Shutterstock; **p113(3)**: ifong / Shutterstock; **p113(4)**: hobo_018 / E+ / Getty Images; **p113(5)**: Buena Vista Images / DigitalVision / Getty Images; **p113(6)**: David Herraez Calzada / Shutterstock; **p116(l)**: 1492 PICTURES / HEYDAY FILMS / WARNER BROS / Album / Alamy Stock Photo; **p116(r)**: Shawshots / Alamy Stock Photo; **p119**: Rocky Prakasit / Shutterstock; **p121**: silviaqs / Shutterstock; **p123**: 80's Child / Shutterstock; **p124**: Vitalii Gaidukov / Shutterstock; **p127**: ecrafts / Shutterstock; **pp128/129**: Helen Hotson / Shutterstock; **p130**: Mr_Twister / iStock / Getty Images Plus / Getty Images; **p134**: Ajdin Kamber / Shutterstock; **p136**: OLGA RYAZANTSEVA / iStock / Getty Images Plus / Getty Images; **p138**: M Rahman / Alamy Stock Photo; **p140**: Alastair Humphreys; **p143**: georgeclerk / E+ / Getty Images; **p144**: Geoff Smith / Alamy Stock Photo; **pp146/147**: Martin Lehmann / Alamy Stock Photo; **p150**: Kumar Sriskandan / Alamy Stock Photo; **pp152/153**: Edwin Remsberg / The Image Bank / Getty Images; **p155**: agefotostock / Alamy Stock Photo; **p156(t)**: Sproetniek / E+ / Getty Images; **p156(m)**: Susana Luzir / Shutterstock; **p156(b)**: Monkey Business Images / Shutterstock; **p157**: Francesco Bergamaschi / Moment / Getty Images; **p158(t)**: Photo12 / Universal Images Group via Getty Images; **p158(b)**: RBM Vintage Images / Alamy Stock Photo; pp158/159(bkg): LOC Photo / Alamy Stock Photo; **p160**: Jack Delano / PhotoQuest/Getty Images; **pp162/163**: Yvette Belcher / Shutterstock.

Artwork by Michael Driver, Geraldine Sy and Kamae Design

Although we have made every effort to trace and contact all copyright holders before publication this has not been possible in all cases. If notified, the publisher will rectify any errors or omissions at the earliest opportunity.

Links to third party websites are provided by Oxford in good faith and for information only. Oxford disclaims any responsibility for the materials contained in any third party website referenced in this work.

MIX
Paper | Supporting responsible forestry
FSC® C007785